TOWARDS AN
ASIAN THEOLOGY

Regnum Series Preface

While we delight to serve the academic community, our mission is to enable the global church to engage more readily in God's mission in its very diverse contexts. To do this we seek to bring practitioners and academics together. Our desire is that this series will bridge the gap that sometimes exists between, on the one hand, Christian leaders and mission practitioners and, on the other, Christian researchers.

About the Author

Hwa Yung was the Bishop of the Methodist Church in Malaysia from 2004-2012. Before that he had served as Principal of Malaysia Theological Seminary, and later as Director, Centre for the Study of Christianity in Asia at Trinity Theological College, Singapore. Over the years he has been closely associated with the Oxford Centre for Mission Studies and the Lausanne Movement. He continues an active preaching and teaching ministry both in and outside Malaysia.

TOWARDS AN
ASIAN THEOLOGY

Hwa Yung

First published 2020 by Regnum Books International

Regnum is an imprint of the Oxford Centre for Mission Studies
St. Philip and St. James Church, Woodstock Road, Oxford, OX2 6HR, UK
www.ocms.ac.uk/regnum

09 08 07 06 05 04 03 8 7 6 5 4 3 2 1

British Library Cataloguing in Publication Data
A catalogue record for this book is available from the British Library

ISBN: 978-1-913363-27-7

Typeset in Palatino by WORDS BY DESIGN
Printed and bound by CPI Group (UK) Ltd, Croydon, CR0 4YY

regnum

CONTENTS

PREFACE

This is an abbreviated version of a book which began its life as a dissertation submitted by Bishop Hwa Yung in Malaysia under the title *Theology and Mission in the Asian Church*. It was then published in 1997 under the title *Mangoes or Bananas?* and republished in 2014. This shortened version is one of a series of Practitioner Books published by Regnum and the Oxford Centre for Mission Studies with the aim of making scholarship easily accessible to busy Christians.

The initial title of the book, *Mangoes or Bananas?* refers to the fruits commonly found in tropical Asia. The banana is of uncertain origins, whereas the mango is an authentic Asian fruit. Ripe bananas are yellow, but when peeled reveal flesh that is off-white in colour. On the other hand, most species of mangoes when ripe are golden yellow on both the outside and the inside. Hwa Yung sees a parable in this comparison. Most of the post-World War Two examples of Asian theology originate from western theological circles and look more like bananas than mangoes – 'yellow' outside, but 'white' inside. Asians may love the banana, but there is no doubt that the sweet, succulent flesh of the mango is prized much more highly. If one has to choose, the latter is much more likely to be preferred. Sadhu Sundar Singh, in the early years of the twentieth century, was deeply convinced that his people needed Christ, the 'Water of Life', but he was equally adamant that 'they do not want it in European vessels but in an Indian cup'.

As an academic, but not a theologian, it has been a privilege to be allowed to edit this book , and I am grateful to Paul Bendor Samuel, Director of Regnum Books, for suggesting it should be done, and to Bishop Hwa Yung for allowing me to do it and for his helpful comments and amendments to my editing.

As it is an abbreviated version of a book first written over 20 years ago, some of the statements may appear to be dated, but it is hoped this will not detract from the major significance of this work.

David Cranston
Oxford Centre for Mission Studies October 2019

In his Preface to the First edition of *Mangoes or Bananas* Hwa Yung wrote

This work is the result of a long pilgrimage which formally began when I first embarked on academic theological studies in Britain some 20 years ago. In some ways I enjoyed my studies then immensely, but in others it was extremely frustrating. On the one hand, it opened my mind and heart to many deep truths of God. On the other, I found that again and again, the western theologies that I was learning often failed to answer the questions that I was consciously and sub-consciously asking from within my own spiritual, cultural, and sociopolitical context. There was a very real sense of disappointment and exasperation in those years.

Later I read more of what Asian theological writers had produced. But again, there was a sense of disappointment with what I found because I felt that much of the material was only superficially contextual. They often failed to really address the questions that the Asian church at the grass-roots was wrestling with. The writings also tended to be too academic. And there was simply too much captivity to the Enlightenment framework.

So I struggled on. At times I almost lost confidence in my own pilgrimage, and despaired of finding genuine answers. For whatever it is worth, this book is the product of that struggle. The task of putting it together has brought me personally some light. I offer it as a contribution to the wider Christian community, in the hope that it will bring some fellow pilgrims, especially those from the Two-Thirds World, some light too.

Hwa Yung
Malaysia Theological Seminary
Petaling Jaya
1996

CHAPTER 1
INTRODUCTION

Over the last few hundred years the Church in the western world has brought the gospel to Africa, Asia and Latin America, but it has done so in a western form. This may have been welcomed in the past by Christians in the two-thirds world, but increasingly this perceived imposition of an alien culture is being questioned and rejected, both from a dissatisfaction of 'western' Christianity and in a quest for a clearer sense of self-identity on the part of Christians throughout the two-thirds world.

Western theologies cannot adequately address the profound differences in the rest of the world. The Asian theologian, Kosuke Koyama, lists six. The relevance of Christ to revolutionary social change; the widespread poverty; the ethnic and economic minorities; the different cultures; the plurality of religions; and the ecclesiastical divisions. While some western writers have worked with these issues, most western theological writings do not deal with them in the same way as those who wrestle with them on a daily basis.

The German theologian, Jürgen Moltmann, a German air force pilot during the Second World War, may have sought in *The Crucified God* a 'theology after Auschwitz' to deal with the problem of evil and suffering. While this might have some appeal for Asian Christians against the background of its political and socio-economic realities, it does not address the six issues that Koyama raises. A wrestling towards a theology after the Rape of Nanjing, or a theology after Hiroshima, would stir up more passionate cords in the Asian context.

The religious worldview of the non-westerner embraces the so called 'high religions', such as Hinduism, Buddhism and Islam, and the 'lower' folk religion of magic, astrology and spirit worship. The western missionary, on the other hand, tends to address only the 'high religions', and in failing to take the non-westerner's worldview seriously, ends up converting others to a western Christianity rather than to a Christianity based in their own culture. At best, this leads to a split-level religion where the rational side of the indigenous Christian's mind is Christianised, but the sub-rational level of consciousness remains pagan. This type of nominal Christianity is prevalent in many parts of the two-thirds world, and, at worst, paves the way for the eventual reversion to various forms of Christo-paganism.

Sensitive Asian Christians are asking for a genuinely indigenous Christian theology that is firmly rooted in the Asian soil, rather than one based on the western worldview in an Asian dress.

THE NEGATIVE IMPACT OF ENLIGHTENMENT THOUGHT AND WESTERN DUALISM

Discussions in mission theology, until very recently, have been dominated by theological ideas from the west. There is little doubt that the main influences that have shaped modern western thought and theology is the European Enlightenment of the seventeenth and eighteenth centuries, and the dualistic tradition in western thought. The latter is rooted in Greek philosophy and the belief that there are two kinds of reality: material (physical) and immaterial (spiritual), separating mind and body from each other.

The Enlightenment was the intellectual and philosophical movement that dominated Europe during the seventeenth and eighteenth centuries. It rejected anything that fell outside rational analysis, and largely disregarded the supernatural.

It was, supremely, the Age of Reason and was initiated by Copernicus (1473-1543), Bacon (1561-1650), Galileo (1564-1642), and others. By the middle or end of the seventeenth century, the Enlightenment worldview had become firmly entrenched. Copernicus, Bacon and others, combined with the rationalism introduced by Descartes, produced a climate in which human reason became the final arbiter of truth. Reason replaced faith, leading to a radical anthropocentrism, leaving no room for God, and questioning the place of the church and its relationship to the world.

To begin with, the European rationalist philosophers of the seventeenth and eighteenth centuries like Descartes (1596-1650) and Spinoza (1632-1677) were concerned to affirm the rationality of the universe and the ability of reason to grasp it. They were not ultimately concerned with debunking faith in God, but some of their ideas paved the way for rationalism, judging everything in light of reason and effectively disposing of the supernatural.

Descartes, the founder of modern philosophy (Cartesian is named after him) resolves to reject anything whose existence can be doubted. Thus he posited his famous *'Cogito, ergo sum'* ('I think, therefore I am') and is seen as the one who made individual self-consciousness the final criterion of truth.

What began as an emphasis on the proper use of reason to understand a rational universe ended up in the elevation of reason into a self-directed principle by which the Christian message is judged and, inevitably, scepticism ensued.

A second stream of Enlightenment thought that has contributed to uncertainty in western theology is the impact of empiricism, the view that the sole source of knowledge comes from observation. This arose in part out of the reaction to philosophical rationalism and its belief that reason was the basis of certain knowledge, David Hume (1711-76) being the best known exponent of this.

Over the years, those who have followed Hume in his narrow interpretation of empiricism have continued to maintain an unwarranted scepticism toward metaphysics and religious belief. Probably the most celebrated example in recent years was Logical Positivism, declaring all statements, apart from purely logical ones, nonsense, unless they can be verified through the senses. By one stroke the Logical Positivists thought they had succeeded in removing all metaphysical and ethical statements from the realm of meaningful discourse, until it was noted that this 'Verification Principle' itself was unverifiable by its own criterion, and therefore is, at best, a piece of 'useful nonsense'.

While few western theologians would identify with the Logical Positivist school, the same sort of commitment to a narrow empiricism has often led to a similar scepticism. Thus miracles are denied because they are perceived to violate scientific laws in a closed universe, an unwarranted assumption to say the least. Concurrently, there is a rejection of much of the historicity of the biblical narratives, and consequently, many of the cardinal doctrines of faith, because they supposedly do not conform to the accepted norms of empirical history. Such a sceptical theology, quite apart from its own inherent weaknesses, is hardly able to address the concerns of the Asian worldview which takes seriously not just metaphysics and theological truths, but also the whole spiritual realm of angels and demons, and the miraculous. This has inevitably shaped western theology and raises the question as to how such a theology can address the concerns of two-thirds world cultures, which look more towards holistic and community concerns and less towards materialism.

Today a fundamental re-evaluation of the Christian faith, free of the assumptions of the modern mentality that are generally hostile to a religious outlook, is called for. As the barriers to the Christian faith erected by the this mentality collapse, both philosophy and science, which were once seen as hostile to religious belief, are now in some respects seen to be pointing the way back to it.

Finally, western theology is often seen as being built on an idealist conception of truth, which distinguishes it from practice. This leads to a theology which is unengaged and, therefore, lacks the power for human and social transformation. The proper view of truth is one which identifies truth with practice, and theology must be historically verified against its conformity to the saving acts of God in the world. Neither theory nor practice may be prioritised over the other. Each is adversely affected when sight is lost of the other. This does not mean that Christians in the two-thirds world necessarily reject western theology but they certainly refuse to accept some aspects of western academic theology.

The perceived unengaged nature of western theology leads to the related perception that it often fails to be relevant in terms of pastoral care or mission outreach. The 1982 Seoul Declaration, 'Towards an Evangelical Theology from the two-thirds world', sums up the problem:

> *Western theology is by and large rationalistic, moulded by western philosophies, preoccupied with intellectual concerns, especially those having to do with the relationship between faith and reason. All too often, it has reduced the Christian faith to abstract concepts which may have answered the questions of the past, but which fail to grapple with the issues of today. It has consciously been conformed to the secularist worldview associated with the Enlightenment. Sometimes it has been utilised as a means to justify colonialism, exploitation, and oppression, or it has done little or nothing to change these situations. Furthermore, having been wrought within Christendom, it hardly addresses the questions of people living in situations characterised by religious pluralism, secularism, resurgent Islam or Marxist totalitarianism.*[1]

These problems have led to the deliberate quest for a theology that would more faithfully express the consciousness of Asian Christianity, and in turn empower Asian Christians for mission in a more effective way.

Asian Theology is used as a broad term to cover the many attempts at expressing the implications of the gospel in the various Asian contexts, from the Indian sub-continent through south-east Asia to Korea and Japan. These include the efforts of different individuals, both past and present, as well as groups of theologians and church leaders with common concerns.

One criterion for assessing the adequacy of Asian theologies is to ask how effectively these theological formulations serve to advance the mission of the church in Asia. This book examines representative examples of Asian theology, both past and present, and assesses their effect. It further outlines the structure of a more adequate Christian theology within an Asian context. Historically, Asian theological reflections have emerged in the context of the mission of the church and the pastoral nurturing of the growth of converts. Surely every theology should ultimately be judged by its efficacy in enhancing or obstructing the mission of Christ, the *missio Dei*.

In the theological writings from the two-thirds world this concern has been raised repeatedly. Thus Latin American liberation theologians criticise traditional western theologies as being unengaged, separating truth and practice, and lacking pastoral and missiological relevance. The same emphasis is also found in the New Testament, for the Bible is not a book about theology as such, but rather, a record of theology in mission, God in action on behalf of the salvation of humanity. Few scholars would deny that the gospels were written to commend Jesus Christ to different audiences in the Graeco-Roman world, and that all the epistles grew out of the pastoral needs of churches in missionary situations. The New Testament records were not written by the equivalent of modern-day scholars with the luxury of leisurely research, but in the context of an 'emergency situation', of a church which, because of its missionary encounter with the world, was forced to nurture theology. Thus mission became the mother of theology.

It is not only in two-thirds world theological writings and in the New Testament that we find the emphasis on theology being pastoral in conception and missional in nature. The nature of theology in the early church was related to the worldview that governed the disposition and practice of believers. This had to be formed through education and nurture. Furthermore, theology was used as the discipline of study, instruction, and shepherding, focusing on understanding, and experiencing the relationship between God and humanity. While this focus could sometimes lead to abstract thought, it was always practical, rooted in the life of the believer. As Augustine puts it, 'The only merit of this science is that from it, a saving faith is born, nourished, defended, and strengthened'.

If theological reflections grew out of the pastoral practices of the early church, it was also further sharpened by the apologetic demands laid upon her. When the church confessed what it believed and taught, it did so in answer to attacks from within and from without the Christian movement. The relations of the church fathers to Judaism and to pagan thought affected much of what they had to say about the various doctrinal issues before them. It is therefore clear that theology in the early church was shaped primarily by pastoral and missiological concerns. All theology was understood as practical, as opposed to merely speculative.

As the social location of the theology switched from the church to the newly emerging universities, theology became separated from its pastoral and mission-based roots and eventually Aquinas' scholastic model of speculative theology took over as the dominant approach to theology.

The Reformation is rightly seen as a repudiation of the medieval scholastic model. Luther took it as self-evident that theology is a practical and not a theoretical science, because the proper study of theology is not God *per se*, but rather the relationship between God and humanity. In the case of Calvin, even in his *Institutes*, he could not be charged with being a speculative theologian because he intended them as a catechism, an apologetic against the false doctrines of his time, and, especially, as an aid to understanding the Bible. The practical orientation of the Reformers was not in system-building but in witnessing to their faith.

Unfortunately for the subsequent development of western theology, the gains made by the Reformers were quickly lost by Protestant orthodoxy, which reverted to the scholastic model under the influence of the universities and the Aristotelian method of critical thinking through deductive reasoning.

At the same time, the influence of Enlightenment led to a separation between theory and practice. Pure or theoretical reason was assumed to be superior to practical reason. This heighten the shift from seeing theology rooted in pastoral and mission-based practice, to systematic theology in the western tradition, largely speculative, and often irrelevant to the mission and pastoral concerns of the church.

This development is an aberration rather than the norm for Christian theology. Not only are the churches of the two-thirds world protesting against it as being an inadequate model for an 'engaged' theology, but it also goes against the Christian understanding and tradition of what theology is in the New Testament, the Patristic and the Reformation periods. Indeed, even in the modern period, there were clear voices of protest in western Christianity, especially in that of John Wesley with his call for a 'practical divinity'.

Furthermore, the most characteristic word for 'knowing' in the Old Testament implies not just comprehension and ability, but also a grasp of what needs to be done. Practical interests are always implied. Edification rather than learning is the main point, and reflective inquiry must be grounded in love and lead to the right action. Truth and practice are not separable and neither can there be knowledge without personal commitment.

Asian thought is not uniform. For example, philosophy in India is never treated as a mere 'intellectual exercise', and truth is not only to be known but also lived. If this is so with India, it is even more true of China. The Chinese have never understood philosophical concepts as intellectual ideas alone, Rather, ideas in Chinese philosophy are always seen in relation to the whole of human existence and culture. The early Confucian classic, *The Great Learning*, exemplifies this clearly:

> *The ancients who wished clearly to exemplify illustrious virtue throughout the world would first set up good government in their states. Wishing to govern well their states, they would first regulate their families. Wishing to regulate their families, they would first cultivate their persons. Wishing to cultivate their persons, they would first rectify their minds. Wishing to rectify their minds, they would first seek sincerity in their thoughts.*

7

Toward an Asian Theology

Wishing for sincerity in their thoughts, they would first extend their knowledge. The extension of knowledge lay in the investigation of things. For only when things are investigated is knowledge extended; only when knowledge is extended are thoughts sincere; only when thoughts are sincere are minds rectified; only when minds are rectified are our persons cultivated; only when our persons are cultivated are our families regulated; only when families are regulated are states well governed; and only when states are well governed is there peace in the world.[2]

Thus, in the Confucian tradition, the goal of the scholar is not just the mastery of the ancient classics, but, ultimately, to become a *junzi*, the 'ideal man', who embodies in one's own person all the truths found therein.

Thus Indian and Chinese minds would never feel at home with a purely speculative theology, which has predominated in western Christianity in the modern period, and to a lesser extent in the medieval period. This is a historical aberration which cannot find support in New Testament practice, and it is being increasingly questioned by Christians from the west as well as by those from non-western cultures.

We conclude, therefore, that there can be no authentic theology that is not properly grounded in the pastoral and mission-based practice of the church, and which does not also demand a personal commitment from the Christian. This being so, it would seem to be justified to assess Asian theological writings on the basis of their competency as theologies of mission.

CHAPTER 2
TOWARD A THEOLOGY OF MISSION

From the Protestant point of view until the beginning of the twentieth century there had been agreement on the definition of mission, and at the First World Missionary Conference at Edinburgh in 1910 there had seemed little need to debate it. However, by the time of the Second World Missionary Conference at Jerusalem in 1928, a shift in thinking had taken place. Many were beginning to look forward to a great synthesis of the world's religions, with secularisation being seen as the great enemy. This movement within ecumenical circles, in a broadly liberal direction, continued through the 1930s, and paved the way for the salvation-or-humanisation debates of the 1960s and 70s, and the exclusivism-inclusivism-pluralism debates of the 1980s and 90s, leading to the evangelical responses which culminated in the Lausanne Movement .

On the Roman Catholic side, there were similarities between pre-Vatican II Roman Catholic mission theology and Protestant theology before Edinburgh 1910. Both affirmed that Jesus Christ is the final revelation of God and the sole source of salvation; and that other religions were at best fallible expressions of humanity's search for the divine, and at worst, demonic deceptions designed to blind us from the truth. The gospel was to be preached to all, and humans would be judged on the basis of their acceptance or rejection of the salvation offered in Christ. Both would emphasise the importance, if not the primacy, of evangelism and the need for incorporation into the institutional church, as well as church planting. Both were equally guilty, in varying degrees, of western cultural imperialism.

However, just as Protestant mission theology has undergone profound changes since Edinburgh, Roman Catholic theology has been going through similar changes in the years since Vatican II (1962-1965), often of a much greater magnitude as it had to simultaneously accommodate the double impact of the Reformation and the Enlightenment. Today the theological battle lines are no longer drawn between Protestants and Catholics as they once were, but they now cut across confessional lines, between the more conservative and the more radical, resulting in certain convergences and divergences in mission theology today.

John Stott notes that two extreme views of mission contributed to the polarisation of the 1960s and 70s. One is the older and more traditional view which focused on the vertical dimension of salvation. It equated mission with evangelism, often focusing entirely on verbal proclamation. At the other extreme is the equally unbiblical view which focused largely on the horizontal dimension of salvation, where mission is defined as humanisation, rather than evangelisation. Now, increasingly, it has come to be accepted by most that mission is a comprehensive concept which includes both the vertical and the horizontal dimensions of salvation.

Despite the different understandings, there is consensus that evangelism and socio-political action are both integral aspects of the goal of mission. Nevertheless, it must be noted that there are still some who would affirm evangelism or socio-political action to the exclusion of the other.

Mission is a comprehensive concept, seen firstly in terms of its *intent*, with the emphasis that the gospel is for all, especially to the poor who are both often deprived of justice as well as neglected in the evangelistic outreach of the church. Secondly it is seen in terms of its *extent*, to all seven continents, with the emphasis is on the continual need for those who have the calling and the gift to cross frontiers to share the gospel of Jesus Christ. Today, instead of the historical one way traffic from the 'north' to the 'south', the emphasis is now on two way traffic, with the disappearance of western dominance in missions and the growing partnership between older and younger churches. Thus the church's mission today is clearly seen to be from each national church to every nation, characterised by the key words partnership, equality, and mutuality.

Furthermore, there is an emphasis on witness to peoples of other faiths and ideologies by The World Council of Churches, Lausanne and the Catholic Church, affirming that the mission to the nations knows no boundaries.

In speaking of witness to peoples of other faiths, all traditions agree that we should respect the views of those of a different religious or ideological persuasion and most would agree that dialogue, as a means of furthering mutual ethical and theological understanding and respect, is right and necessary. Where Christians differ is in their assessment of the value of non-Christian religions in leading to salvation.

Lausanne's position on this is unambiguous. It affirms that, 'we... reject as derogatory to Christ and the gospel every kind of syncretism and dialogue which implies that Christ speaks equally through all religions and ideologies and we have no warrant for saying that salvation can be found outside Christ (John 14:6)'. The position of the World Council of Churches is less clear, stating, 'We cannot point to any other way of salvation than Jesus Christ; at the same time we cannot set limits to the saving power of God.'

The exact position of the Roman Catholic Church is a matter of debate today. Pope John Paul II in *Redemptoris Missio* was unambiguous that, 'Christ is the one Savior of all, the only one able to reveal God and lead to God.' But many commentators of Vatican II have maintained that, although it does not explicitly affirm other religions as means of divine revelation and salvation, that is nevertheless its intention. Despite its unprecedented respect of other religions, Vatican II maintains the uniqueness of God's revelation and salvation in Christ. The flashes of truth found in other faiths need to be purified and perfected by the fullness of God's revelation in Christ and entrusted to the church.

Both the Roman Catholic Church and Lausanne agree that the church is at the centre of God's cosmic purpose and is his appointed means of spreading the gospel. Moreover, we are to work towards greater co-operation and unity so as to reflect the oneness which Christ prayed for (John 17:20f), in order that the world might believe.

There is now a clear consensus that much more effort must be made to root the gospel in indigenous cultures. The church needs to repent of the cultural imperialism of the past era that has often hindered younger churches from being properly implanted in their cultural soil. 'Missions have all too frequently exported an alien culture with the gospel, and churches have sometimes been in bondage to culture rather than to Scripture.'[3] The gospel does not affirm the superiority of any culture over another.

In its discussion on conversion and culture, Lausanne's 'Willowbank Report' draws attention to the need of a 'power encounter', wherein Christ is shown to be the Lord of the powers.

This may seem strange to the secularised western mind, and probably explains why this issue has been omitted in much present-day discussion on inculturation. But as the report states,

> *those from Asia, Africa, and Latin America, have spoken both of the reality of evil powers and of the necessity to demonstrate the supremacy of Jesus over them. For conversion involves a power encounter. People give their allegiance to Christ when they see that his power is superior to magic and voodoo, the curses and blessings of witch doctors, and malevolence of evil spirits, and that his salvation is a real liberation from the power of evil and death.*[4]

This is a matter that deserves more serious attention than has thus far been given to it in discussions on mission. If we are truly concerned about both gospel and culture, and the interrelation between them, we must take non-western worldviews seriously.

THE ROOTS OF DIVERGENCES IN MISSION THEOLOGY: THE ENLIGHTENMENT AND WESTERN DUALISM

These two influences, the Enlightenment and western dualism, have combined to produce a climate of scepticism that hampers the genuine expression of biblical faith. They have led to the centrality of individualism and accentuating the individualisation of salvation, a tendency which has been endemic in western theology since Augustine, giving primary emphasis to the redemption of the soul rather than the reconciliation of the world.

Furthermore, the Enlightenment functioned with a subject-object distinction, separating humanity from the rest of nature, suggesting that nature could be fully evaluated and analysed and giving humanity an unprecedented sense of confidence and boldness over the rest of the world, with permission to exploit it if necessary.

This separation between subject and object in the natural sciences soon came to be applied in theology as well. This was especially so in the critical study of the Bible, wherein the text was treated objectively like any other human document. At the heart of the matter was both a religious and psychological difficulty, asking whether the Bible could be both an object of critical studies and the channel of God's revelation at one and the same time. In reality this allowed scholars to question the text, but not to be questioned by it, leading to conflict between reason and the authority of the Bible.

A further characteristic of the Enlightenment made nature an object of study and thus paved the way for the introduction of nature as a direct cause and the means for understanding reality, eliminating the idea of any purpose or reason in science, This led to the mechanistic view of a closed and deterministic universe, which supposedly could be completely understood once all the natural laws were discovered. This in turn contributed to the rejection of the miraculous and supernatural, which by definition could not happen in a closed mechanistic universe.

This resultant cause-effect mode of thinking also implied that, as long as the right conditions were met, the success of any project, including the missionary enterprise, was guaranteed. This was one source of the debate on whether evangelism or social action had priority in mission, which eventually contributed to the growing rift between liberals and conservatives in this area.

The new scientific advances, coupled with the discovery of the New World (as Europeans understood it) and the beginning of the modern colonial era, led to humanity's increasing sense of confidence that they had both the ability and the will to remake the world in their own image. This confidence in human progress expressed itself in the belief in technological development and modernisation, and added to the superiority felt by western civilisation over others. For Christians, this optimism was expressed in the belief that the spread of Christian knowledge would lead eventually to worldwide evangelism, social progress and justice. Increasingly, the Kingdom of God became identified with western culture and civilisation.

This gave rise to the sense of both religious and cultural superiority felt by missionaries and explained why Christian missions were often so closely identified with colonialism in the nineteenth and twentieth centuries. More importantly, it also explains why the attempt to set the gospel within its cultural context made little progress in the same period, despite the fact that most Protestant missionary societies had adopted 'indigenisation', with Henry Venn's concept of 'self-governing, self-supporting, and self-propagating churches', as their official policy.

Another characteristic of Enlightenment thinking was the distinction between 'fact' and 'value'. In an empirically defined world based on observation and experience, what may be considered 'facts' belong to the realm of the scientifically-testable. A belief is true only to the extent that it corresponds with facts. According to Karl Popper, this means that knowledge in an objective sense is totally independent of anyone's belief or claims to knowing. 'Facts', therefore, are public, in contrast to 'values', which are based on privately-held opinions and beliefs. Consequently, the latter, which includes religious beliefs, cannot lay claim to being true or false, because these are supposedly mere matters of private choices, based on subjective preferences.

Among other things, it led to the gradual separation between the secular and religious, as the Enlightenment banished religion to the private realm, leaving the public realm to reason. This further contributed to the subsequent split in mission theology between social transformation and evangelism.

The Enlightenment gave rise to the confidence that 'all problems were in principle solvable'. Humanity had, as it were, come of age. There were no gaps or mysteries which could resist discovery by the human mind. This affirmation, together with the belief in a mechanistic universe, eradicated all that was miraculous or scientifically inexplicable. There was, therefore, no place for belief in the healing ministry of the church, or the personal demonic dimension in life, and increasingly, there was not even a place for God.

Humanity was now regarded as a society of emancipated, autonomous individuals, with an optimistic faith in human nature, in contrast to Augustinian and Reformation doctrines. All were free to pursue their happiness and to do so without restraints. This gave rise to a rampant individualism, where the church, and eventually the Bible, became peripheral and everyone was free to believe what he or she wished and to choose accordingly.

The net result of all this is that the universe is perceived in dualistic categories at every point: the individual mind and the external world, soul and body, spirit and matter, subject and object, fact and value, religious and secular. The consequences of this on mission thinking are plain. Instead of holistic thinking, one asks if salvation is spiritual or physical and socio-political. Is the soul more important or the body? Is it evangelisation or humanisation? Does God work in the physical realm or does he act only in the spiritual realm? If he acts only in the latter, then any changes in the physical realm can only come about by human efforts, presumably socio-political action. But if he works also in the physical realm, then miracles and healing can occur.

The overall consequences of dualism and the Enlightenment for mission theology paved the way for the modern debates on whether the intent of mission is evangelisation or socio-political action. The deistic view of a closed mechanistic universe, which is built upon a dualistic separation between spirit and matter, effectively ruled out the place of miraculous healing and the ministry of exorcism from the missiological agenda of the church. The scepticism which resulted from Cartesian dualism that exalts doubt over faith led not only to an undermining of divine revelation and a loss of the authority of the Bible, but it also opened the flood-gates for the widespread denial of Christian truth, as demonstrated by the pluralism debate.

The secularisation of the church and the world in modern thought, together with the increasing anthropocentrism in theology, combined to force the agenda, with its concern to replace evangelisation with humanisation as the goal of mission, and its determination to blur the identity of the church. Finally, with the presumption that modernity built upon the Enlightenment model represents the zenith of humanity's coming of age, there is little wonder why there existed the unspoken tendency to equate the Kingdom of God with western civilisation and consequently, the lack of serious attention given to the application of the gospel in non-western contexts by western missions in general.

TOWARD A THEOLOGY OF MISSION
It is now increasingly recognised that the thinking that has contributed to shaping western thought in general, and mission theology in particular, has been found wanting. All this is not to suggest that the contributions of the western intellectual tradition and the Enlightenment are entirely negative. It has led to many real advances in human knowledge, such as the use of logic, critical reasoning, and the empirical method. But western dualism and Enlightenment thought are far from adequate as foundations upon

which to build a sound intellectual and theological framework in the postmodern world. In fact, Karl Barth was probably the first significant western theologian to realise this, attempting to construct a theology that rose above the problems caused both by Greek dualism and Enlightenment thought. Whether he succeeded or not is another question.

But the existing divergences in mission theology, rooted as they are in dualistic and Enlightenment categories, can no longer be taken with the same seriousness as they once were. Consequently, we should now be able to define the theology of mission with greater clarity. The purpose of mission is comprehensive, with both horizontal and vertical dimensions. This means that it should include evangelism *and* church planting, deliverance from diseases *and* demon powers, as well as socio-political action for freedom *and* justice in the world, empowering the church to carry out its God-given mission, within its own context.

However, a theology of mission must not only be concerned with making itself relevant to a particular context. It must also at the same time be concerned with being faithful to the unchanging core of beliefs which it is trying to make relevant, thus ensuring that it is faithful to the Christian tradition which it is attempting to make relevant in a particular context.

CHAPTER 3

CRITERIA FOR A MISSION-BASED THEOLOGY –
PART ONE

Andrew Walls is a British historian of missions, best known for his pioneering studies of the history of the African church. He writes that one unchanging feature in Christian history is:

> *the desire to 'indigenise', to live as a Christian and yet as a member of one's own society, to make the church ... 'A place to feel at home'. The desire to do this is tied up with the very nature of the gospel;* it is patterned in the Incarnation itself *(emphasis mine). When God became man, Christ took flesh in a particular family, members of a particular nation, with the tradition of customs associated with that nation. All that was not evil he sanctified. Wherever he is taken by men in any time and place he takes that nationality, that society, that 'culture', and sanctifies all that is capable of sanctification by his presence ... No group of Christians has therefore any right to impose in the name of Christ upon another group of Christians a set of assumptions about life determined by another time and place.*[5]

This he calls the 'indigenising' principle.

However, there is the constant danger of over-reaction, wherein the attempt to live and study theology from within one's own context leads to a clean break with one's Christian theological ancestry. In affirming the contextual nature of all theology, we need also to affirm that which transcends the context. Secondly, we need to guard against the problem of western theology in the past wherein western theological formulations were elevated to the status of absolute divine truth before which all other peoples and cultures must bow. There must not be a tendency amongst two-thirds world theologians to repeat the same mistake of their western counterparts.

Secondly what Andrew Walls has also called the 'pilgrim' principle must always be held in tension with the 'indigenising' principle, for God does not just take us as where we are and leave us there. He seeks to transform us into what he wants us to be. Here the Christian has no abiding city and to be faithful to Christ will put him out of step with his society; for no society ever existed, in east or west, ancient time or modern, which could absorb the word of Christ painlessly into its system. It is when we are able to keep in proper tension both these principles, that we can then hold together the particulars of our contexts and the universal nature of the gospel without losing sight of either.

During the colonial period, most scientists assumed that scientific theories were accurate descriptions of the world as it is in itself. Many missionaries adopted the same view of theology, and assumed that western theology, properly crafted, was absolutely true. Since other religions and cultures were at best partial reflections of the truth, the task of the missionaries was merely to implant the same theology unchanged in the mission fields.

CONTEXTUALISATION AND SOCIO-POLITICAL CONCERNS
However, a truly Asian theology must come to terms with the needs of the peoples of the continent, and one key criterion of an adequate theology of mission would be whether it is able to speak to the physical and social needs of humanity in a situation wherein poverty, political and economic injustice, ethnic, ideological and national divisions, and oppression of all forms prevail. This is an unspoken assumption of the various forms of liberation theology that have been emerging in Latin America, South Africa, Asia and elsewhere since the 1970s.

Nevertheless, there are those on the more theologically conservative side who are still not fully persuaded of this. For them, socio-political action is seen as a distraction or even a betrayal of evangelism, arguing that the New Testament documents provide no sanctions for Christian socio-political involvement. Yet recent studies have made it abundantly clear that this can no longer be sustained from the Biblical texts. The principle of responsible citizenship is so clearly emphasised therein that it must express itself in socio-political involvement today, and the teachings and values espoused by Jesus and his followers posed a serious threat to the existing socio-political order of the day. Similarly, the social stance of the church in Acts was such that, if it were given enough time to recruit new members and to transmit its values and practices, the Roman empire could not avoid serious disruption.

Historically, the hesitation to identify socio-political concerns as one aspect of the mission of the church is traceable to the modernist-fundamentalist debates. In the American scene, in particular, it became increasingly difficult to hold together both revivalism, with its strong evangelistic emphasis, and socio-political concerns. But the real roots of the problem are ultimately to be found in dualism on the one hand, and the individualisation and spiritualisation of salvation on the other.

It should be clear that we need to move beyond the inherent separation of evangelism and socio-political concerns, and to see these as dimensions of the one indivisible mission of the church. Moreover, as John Stott has argued, even if the Great Commission (Matt 28:18-20) relates exclusively to evangelism, a doubtful premise in itself, it must nevertheless be held together with the Great Commandment (Mark 12:31) in our understanding of the church's mission. And Christian love cannot be reduced to evangelism alone, but must find concrete expressions in midst of the socio-political realities of life.

There are different levels of socio-political involvement. At the first level, we have social advocacy, which is limited to involvement at the verbal and written level only, without active participation in the real world. At the second and third levels are respectively social concerns, which seek to alleviate immediate needs and suffering, and socio-political action, which aims at transforming oppressive structures. Both of these require active involvement in the world. Unfortunately, many writers on socio-political concerns rarely go beyond the first level. While Latin American liberation theology represents the clearest articulation of the attempt to address in theological terms the socio-political context in the two-thirds world, Asian Christians have in recent years also begun to do the same. The latter's efforts do not merely repeat the former's ideas, but add their uniquely Asian contributions to the discussions.

Biblical liberation involves socio-political liberation, freedom from personal and psychological bondages, and above all from the root problem of sin. But many who advocate liberation theology put the political above everything else. Malcolm Muggeridge, a British journalist and himself a convert from Marxism, asks rhetorically, 'How many liberations are celebrated that only led to new servitudes! … How many liberators were installed in power only to become more ferocious tyrants than those they replaced'.[6]

This of course raises the all important question as to whether it is possible to bring about genuine liberation without direct evangelism that leads to repentance from sin, freedom from the power of sin and Satan, and the appropriation of the Holy Spirit's power in human affairs.

CONTEXTUALISATION AND THE CHURCH'S EVANGELISTIC AND PASTORAL MINISTRIES

Evangelism could best be defined as 'that set of intentional activities which is governed by the goal of initiating people *into the kingdom of God* (my italics) for the first time'.[7] It must necessarily be a multi-dimensional activity involving many things, including proclamation, acts of mercy, prayer, teaching, and exorcism. Initiation into the kingdom must necessarily be followed by initiation into the church. Hence, church growth is a necessary concomitant of evangelism. Pastoral ministry logically follows evangelism and is the means of nurturing Christian individuals and communities to maturity of faith, life and witness in Christ.

A truly contextual theology must be able to enhance the church's evangelistic and pastoral ministries. To do so, it must first take the evangelistic and pastoral tasks of the church seriously. It must then help the church to find the means to go about these tasks in a relevant manner, adapting the ministry sensitively to the indigenous culture of the people with whom one is working. At times this will involve a holistic approach to evangelism which links it to some form of socio-political action.

The ministries of healing and exorcism, having been neglected for some time by the church at large, are slowly forcing their way back into the mission agenda of the worldwide church in part due to their 'rediscovery' as part of the heritage of the church's total ministry by modern-day Pentecostals and others. What are we to make of this phenomenon of 'signs and wonders'?

In the last two or three centuries, western Christianity's understanding of this matter has been seriously crippled by its Enlightenment and dualistic presuppositions of a closed mechanistic universe which left no room for divine healing and for God, let alone the devil. In contrast to this, the New Testament is replete with examples of divine healing and exorcism. Further, it is now increasingly being recognised that 'signs and wonders' have been practiced in the church throughout her history, and what is supposedly being 'rediscovered' in western Christianity has always been part and parcel of the Christian practice in the two-thirds world. This is certainly true of some of the Asian Christian leaders of previous generations, including Pastor Hsi (c.1835-1896) and John Sung (1901-1944) of China, and Sadhu Sundar Singh (1889-c.1929) of India.

It is also present during periods of spiritual revival in churches such as Kurt Koch's (1971) account of the Indonesian revivals in the 1960s, and Shirley Lees' report (1979) of revivals in Borneo (East Malaysia). Jonathan Chao notes that this is one of the key factors contributing to evangelism and church growth in China. The same holds true in Latin America and Africa. Why then should we be so hesitant to affirm the supernatural?

Paul Hiebert (1932-2007) was an American missiologist who wrote out of his experiences in India, entitled *The Flaw of the Excluded Middle*, where he argues that the western mind has a blind spot which makes it difficult for it to understand, let alone deal with, problems related to astrology, ancestors and spirits. He argues that the western mind has a two-tiered view of reality. The upper level deals with theistic answers to life, and rational beliefs concerning God and other beings who act in the spiritual (and other) world. The lower level is that of the empirical sciences which perceives this world as being controlled by lifeless and impersonal forces. In contrast, the Indian and biblical worldviews consist of three tiers. The upper and lower tiers are similar, at least formally if not materially, to that of the west. However, there is also a middle level of 'Folk or Low Religion' which consists of beliefs in the local deities, ancestral and other spirits, demons, astrology, and the like who or which act in this world. As this middle level is absent in the western mind, western theology has little or no answers for the problems arising here.

Paul Hiebert's thesis finds strong support in the writings and ministry of the former Roman Catholic Archbishop Milingo of Zambia. For Milingo, the world 'below' and the world 'above' are the worlds where humans and God dwell respectively. But the 'world in-between' is the spirit world where the two other worlds meet, and where God actively intervenes. Milingo interprets his ministry of healing and exorcism, which he sees as entirely biblical, within this analytical framework. Another African theologian, Osadolor Imasogie, has also emphasised the need to take seriously the spirit world in the African worldview in the development of a truly African Christian theology.

This leads to the related question of the reality or otherwise of the 'principalities and powers'. It is obviously impossible to deal with this adequately here. What can be safely affirmed is that, first, whereas it was fashionable in the earlier half of this century in western theological circles to reject any serious belief in Satan or demons, and to completely demythologise or de-spiritualise the 'powers', this is no longer the case today. There are clear examples of a renewed wrestling with this issue in theological circles today. Secondly, the reality of Satan and demons is assumed throughout the New Testament. One simply cannot make proper sense of Jesus or Paul's ministries of exorcism, and, to a lesser extent, healing, without that presupposition. Thirdly, as noted earlier, the ministries of exorcism and healing are being reemphasised throughout the Christian world today. Taken together, these factors increasingly force us to the conclusion that Hiebert's critique, that the western worldview is flawed because of the 'excluded middle', has implications beyond missions in the two-thirds world. (This reference to the 'excluded middle' will be discussed throughout this book in relations to those who have sought to present an Asian theology.) Ultimately, we need to ask, are worldviews which include this component more accurate descriptions of reality than those which exclude it? For, if our worldviews miss out on some dimension of reality, we will fail to bring the gospel to bear on that aspect of reality. The extent to which we fail to do so, is the extent to which the gospel will fail to be truly liberating.

This leads to the fourth important issue. A cursory survey of much that today goes by the name Asian theology (or, for that matter, African or Latin American theology) hardly, if ever, touches on this realm of reality. Here we see clearly the debilitating influence of the western Enlightenment and dualism on Asian theological writings. Most of these have so neglected the 'excluded middle' from their considerations that it gives rise to the question whether they adequately understand, let alone address, Asian realities.

Thus if Asian theology is to be truly contextual, it must first be able to empower the church in its evangelistic task of bringing persons to repentance and faith in Christ, and into the kingdom of God. Secondly, it must be able to facilitate the pastoral ministry of the church including church-planting and growth, and the nurture and teaching of disciples to maturity in faith. Thirdly, a contextual theology will be such that it will be able to do the above tasks in a manner which takes Asian cultures and worldviews seriously. This would necessarily involve the practice of 'power encounters' in the healing and exorcism ministries, with serious attention being given to inculturation. Finally, as a logical concomitant of the above, it must be able to empower the Asian church in apostolic cross-cultural missions to other peoples.

CONTEXTUALISATION AND INCULTURATION

The term 'inculturation', rather than 'contextualisation' is increasingly being used to describe this concern for culture and it is of Roman Catholic origins. Thus, instead of an external relationship between the gospel and culture, it urges a dynamic 'ongoing process of reciprocal interaction',[8] 'suggesting a *double movement*: there is at once inculturation of Christianity and Christianisation of culture'.[9]

Worldviews

The fact that Asian worldviews tend to be holistic, rather than dualistic, has important consequences for the communication of the gospel in Asia. This may be illustrated by China's response to the gospel in the twentieth century. Despite China's strong xenophobic fear of foreigners and history of persistent rejection of Christianity, the gradual collapse of the old China in the nineteenth century and the loss of confidence in the ancient traditions led to a great openness to the gospel at the beginning of the twentieth century. Then in the 1920s a strong anti-Christian reaction set in among the intellectuals which stifled the growth of the church once more.

There were already a number of historical and cultural reasons which had predisposed the Chinese against Christianity. One of the key reasons appears to be that the gospel was presented in dualistic terms to a culture that invariably thought and functioned holistically. China was looking for deliverance from colonial oppression by western powers and Japan, and from its economic and industrial backwardness. The conservatives presented a gospel which promised salvation for the soul but not for the body or the nation. The Chinese intellectual leadership rejected that as mere superstition and irrelevant to their struggle for national salvation. On the other hand, the modernists did bring a gospel of social salvation which included modern education, technology and medicine. Why did China not accept this version of Christianity? The answer probably is partly to be found in the failure of liberal Christianity, with its secularised worldview, to take seriously the spiritual dimension in the Chinese worldview. It failed to provide a distinctive answer to the moral quest of the Chinese mind for a spiritual renewal in the individual, without which national reconstruction could not occur. Thus, both the conservatives and the liberals sought to present the message of Christ, but each presented half the gospel at best. The result was that both truncated versions of the gospel were rejected because the felt needs of a holistic culture were not properly met.

Ways of Thinking
The west, India and China represent three different ways of knowing, which can be illustrated by the question of the veracity of reported miracles. The western mind asks, 'How can miracles be possible in a scientific age?' The Chinese mind asks, 'Can I trust the person who reportedly witnessed and told me of the miracle?' The Indian mind asks, 'I will accept its truthfulness if I can experience it for myself.' This ends up shaping the theological questions asked and the approaches taken from within each culture.

Closely related to this is the matter of patterns of logic. On the basis of an analysis of logical patterns in linguistic structures, Robert B. Kaplan has suggested that the patterns of logic in English (Anglo-American), Semitic (Middle-Eastern) and Oriental cultures can be represented by the diagrams in Figure 1.

In our efforts to communicate the gospel cross-culturally in Asia, we must take seriously the differing ways of thinking. Thus the preference for non-linear logic among Chinese, Japanese and other east Asians, allows for much more emphasis to be given to stories, parables, pictures, narratives, poetry, and songs, instead of rational apologetics and systematic theologies build upon cold analytical approaches to biblical studies. On the other hand, rational apologetics will seem to be necessary among some Indians, whose Hindu or Buddhist backgrounds have already familiarised them with analytical logic.

Fig 1 – Patterns of Logic[10]

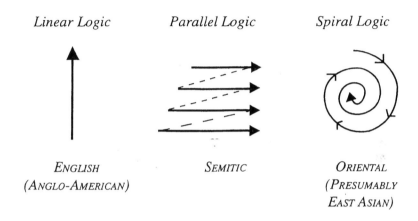

Linear Logic	Parallel Logic	Spiral Logic
ENGLISH (ANGLO-AMERICAN)	SEMITIC	ORIENTAL (PRESUMABLY EAST ASIAN)

Family and Group Solidarity

Family solidarity is one attribute that characterises virtually all Asian cultures, other than western-educated individuals. The family is not only the primary social group, but it is also the model of all social organisations. Generally, families in the traditional Asian setting are complex, rather than nuclear. It is common for kinship to extend beyond the complex family through cousin-marriages, thus creating a whole interlocking network of wider family relationships within a village or, indeed, a larger geographical area.

Within such societies the question of the place of the individual relative to the group is not always easily defined. In Chinese society, Confucian ethics treats the individual and the family as equally important and mutually dependent.

The emphasis on family and group solidarity in Asian cultures has clear implications for contextualisation. For example traditional western-style evangelism presupposes the priority of the individual over the group. The western model of youth evangelism, for example, is based on a cultural model in which youths are given a fair degree of freedom to make their own choices. This rarely occurs, even in cosmopolitan Asian cities. The cultural emphasis on families require Asian Christians to focus on evangelistic methods that are much more family and group-orientated, and to begin with the heads of families or communities. There are clear evidences that these are more fruitful than approaches which presuppose a western individualism.

A second example concerns ethics. Christian moral thinking formulated in the west prioritises principles above relationships. But how do Christian ethics operate in a culture where the order is reversed? For example, family ties are so close in many Asian societies that nepotism invariably results. Yet, if a Christian fails to 'take care' of family members, he or she is also damned in the eyes of his or her culture. Or again, where is the dividing line to be drawn between a bribe and a gift given in appreciation and to cement a relationship? There is obviously a need for the development of a more culturally sensitive ethics.

The third example concerns pastoral practice. For example, theological discussions on infant baptism invariably centres on biblical, historical and theological questions. But could the real issue be the cultural one of how God's covenant with us is worked out in different cultures some presupposing individual decisions and others family and group decisions?

Guilt and/or Shame Consciousness

We come next to the question of guilt and shame, which has often been a source of real frustration to western missionaries. Shame is a reaction to other people's criticism, while guilt is internal. However, it must be asked whether such a distinction can be absolute, or should they rather be seen as relative tendencies, since most, if not all, cultures have the concepts of both guilt and shame. The advent of Buddhism introduced the concept of guilt into Japan. Although modern-day Japanese are noticeably lacking in sin-consciousness in its religious sense, they are very shame-conscious in its practical and moral sense, because conformity to their particular social group is a cultural necessity.

Chinese culture, with its strong emphasis on the importance of *li*, or rules of propriety which covers all aspects of life – personal, social and religious – obviously possesses a strong sense of shame-consciousness, but a guilt or sin-consciousness is almost universally lacking.

However there is a universality of the moral conscience and the concept of guilt in all cultures. Whether they are from a guilt or shame culture, 'people are aware of wrongdoing (though they may not call it sin) and they try to justify themselves and/or find some sort of atonement'.[11] Thus, the problems that western missionaries have had in trying to instil a sense of sin into indigenous believers may in fact arise from the efforts of the former in trying to impose a universal definition of sin (which is in reality a western cultural interpretation) upon the latter.

How can we help those from shame cultures to come to a clear understanding and conviction of sin in the Christian sense? This is important because when the meaning of sin is not properly communicated, what is heard in the call to repentance in Christ is the turning from shameful things instead of sinful things, which can be quite different. First, we must avoid imposing a western ethics upon another culture, and to demand surface changes which may be quite unnecessary. Second, we will need to carefully analyse the culture in which we are working so that we can get below the surface to the underlying moral values and meanings. Third, we should begin speaking about repentance in those areas in which the Holy Spirit is already convicting in the culture. Fourth, we should urge Christians in non-western cultures to read the Bible for themselves from within their own cultures, and to trust the Holy Spirit to lead them to develop a Christian ethic for their own cultures. Careful attention to these will make it easier for those in shame cultures to understand the gospel in its totality.

Concepts of Authority and Leadership Patterns
Self-government is a precondition for the development of a truly indigenous church. But for self-government to be effective and Christian at the same time, the patterns of church leadership must be developed in proper association between gospel and culture, taking into account Asian concepts of authority and leadership.

In contrast to western leadership models which are largely institutional and democratic in nature, in the Asian situation they are more personalised, paternalistic and authoritarian. In general Asian cultures link authority to virtue, but the brutal use of intimidation, with an associated breakdown of law and order, is an ever-lurking danger. Any relaxation of authority is seen as dangerous, and therefore authoritarianism is much more readily accepted than in the west.

A second aspect is the type of persons in whom authority resides. It is a well-known fact that in China moral authority and power is vested with the scholar-gentlemen and, as in every traditional Asian culture, age is respected. In India, spiritual authority is vested in the *guru* who may be a monk or a *sannyasin*, the wandering holy man, who adopts a life of renunciation. This is often associated with the fourth and final stage of life in classical Hinduism; the earlier stages being firstly spiritual training, secondly marriage and establishment of a family and then thirdly, life as a forest hermit. Thus, in both cases, moral and spiritual authority lies with the elderly who have undergone education and self-cultivation.

Within Asian churches, distaste for open criticism of authority, fear of upsetting the unity of the community, and knowledge that any violation of the community's rules of propriety will lead to ostracism, all combine to limit the appeal of western democracy. Furthermore, it is arguable that the influence of the western seminary approach to training has led to an over-emphasis on the academic preparation of Asian church leadership at the expense of the moral and spiritual. If Asian theology is to be truly contextual, it must help the churches to rethink their authority patterns, and ways of choosing and training leaders. In particular, it must focus on the question of how Asian cultural characteristics on the one hand, and the biblical emphases of spiritual and moral maturity, and knowledge of Christian truths on the other, can be brought into creative tension with each other to produce the desired kind of leader for the Asian church.

Understanding of History
The Christian view of history is founded on three convictions: that God acts in it, that he guides it in a uni-linear direction, and that he will bring history to his intended goal. This is rather different from the Indian and Chinese view of history, which have been described as cyclical, but not in the same sense. Indian thought conceives the universe of going through cycles or *Mahayuga* of some 12,000 years.

Human life is caught in endless cycles, and that human activity is in the final analysis futile because what has been will always be. This view of history and of life is reinforced by the doctrines of *karma* and *samsara* as applied to individual lives, which stress the endless cycles of birth and rebirth from which all Hindus and Buddhists strive to escape. This is a world of impermanence – human effort here and now is futile, and resignation becomes the prescription for life. Cosmic cycles breed passivity.

The Chinese view of history is built on the concept of dynastic cycles. The central concept is that of the 'mandate of heaven' being given to the first ruler of a dynasty as a reward for his virtue, and forfeited by the last because of moral failure. History provides a store-house of precedents to guide current ethical and political practice. The Chinese world view is thus transformational rather than cyclical.

How is the gospel to impact Asian cultures, given the very different worldviews of history? With respect to the Indian view of history, while we may grant that there are certain cyclical patterns in human existence, Christianity nevertheless affirms a direction in history, which humanity can help fulfil. It is precisely at this point that the gospel challenges the Indian worldview and its concomitant passivity in this life.

Similarly, in the case of the Chinese view of history, although it has a transformational function, it remains focused on a past antiquity rather than on the future. There is no clear future goal towards which history is moving. This appears to be the key reason why China in the past has always tended to lock itself into an antiquated conservatism from which it is only recently emerging. It remains the task of Christian theology to show that the gospel can contribute towards the preservation of the deepest yearnings of China's ancient traditions, without allowing the culture to be entrapped by these in a manner that is hostile to progress at the same time.

On the other hand, Japan's adaptation to the modern world may have fuelled western theories that industrialisation has led to the disappearance of the cultural distinctiveness of Asian societies and so one should not worry about inculturation. The historical Japanese family structure is based on *samurai* practice and legally codified at the beginning of the Meiji period (1868-1913). Its chief characteristic is the household, the *ie*, which was a continuing unit consisting of a single married couple in each generation remaining in the home, with several generations living and working together as a unit and putting the concerns of the unit above individual interests.

After the end of the Second World War, the *ie* as a legal entity was abolished in preference for the western model of the nuclear family, assuming this would bring Japanese family structure in line with western ones. However, at both the village and urban levels, the *ie* often remains the basic unit for social, political and religious life.

The same observation applies to the impact of modernisation on religious faith. Many changes and adaptations to the religious practices of the Japanese people have occurred, leading to merging of beliefs of all sorts. Thus, typically, a supposedly irreligious Japanese may have participated in Shinto shrines as a child, undergone a Shinto or Christian wedding, lived by Confucian or Christian morality, sought help from 'shamanistic-type' healers, and attended Buddhist funeral services. But that has not resulted in a secularisation of Japanese society nor prevented them from retaining their cultural distinctives in religion.

Other examples can be found in the resurgence of the pursuit of tribal, ethnic, national and religious identity throughout the world today. Even in cosmopolitan Singapore, one of the most westernised of Asian societies, there is a resurgence of Chinese traditions following the government's call in the 1980s for a reemphasis on Confucian values to give a moral underpinning to Singapore society. That being so, the agenda for the inculturation of the gospel in Asia is one that the Asian churches cannot escape.

CHAPTER 4

CRITERIA FOR A MISSIOLOGICAL THEOLOGY – PART TWO

CONTEXTUALISATION AND FAITHFULNESS TO THE CHRISTIAN TRADITION

It is now being argued that what is normative in the gospel should be defined by 'classical Christianity', in contrast to the more liberal attitudes shaped by the Enlightenment, where doubt is promoted above faith, and relativism above truth.

The ancient ecumenical consensus of Christianity's first millennium was built upon faithfulness to canonical scripture and formulated at the seven Ecumenical Councils affirmed by Catholic, Protestant and Orthodox traditions. Such an understanding of the heart of the gospel would also accord with the famous canon of Vincent of Lerins that the Catholic faith is, 'that which has been believed everywhere, always and by all'. These doctrinal affirmations, which include the Nicene Creed and the Chalcedonian Definition, are not the work of isolated individuals but were hammered out by Christians meeting on a worldwide basis.

But this presupposes that we can have a definitive knowledge of God and take seriously the idea of propositional revelation – that is, that God does reveal definitive truths about himself and his ways with humanity. How else can we by ourselves have true knowledge about God?

If God has intended to reveal himself to us in order that we may know him and the way of salvation, and experience moral growth, how else can he do so without revealing some information about himself, his provision for our atonement, and his moral demands on his creatures? That being the case, there can be no alternative to humanity's need for propositional revelation.

Of course both the creeds and scripture come to us in an inculturated form and, therefore, need to be reinterpreted by the church in every generation and culture to ensure continuity with the original revelation. However, the heart of the gospel is not something that can be changed at will into something that is entirely different from what was given. Rather, it is the norm to which all theologies must remain faithful and by which they must be judged.

CONTEXTUALISATION AND FAITHFULNESS TO THE CHRISTIAN TRADITION: A CRITIQUE OF RELIGIOUS PLURALISM

What is Religious Pluralism?
Present day debates on religious exclusivism, inclusivism and pluralism are not new. From the western theological viewpoint, they can be traced back to earlier efforts from the latter part of the nineteenth century onwards, to come to terms with the dawning realisation of the religious diversity in the world. These responses can be summed up as, 'All religions are relative, essentially the same and have common psychic origins'.

While exclusivism accepts that the central claims of Christianity as true, and other religions, in areas of disagreement are false, inclusivism adopts a positive view of other religions and allows for God's saving action through other religions.

'Pluralism' distinguishes itself from exclusivism and inclusivism by denying any uniqueness to God's revelation or saving act in Christ. The Christian faith is merely one of many equally legitimate human responses to the same divine reality. It stands together with all other religious faiths as one of the many equally valid paths to 'God' or ultimate reality.

The implication of pluralism is that Christians must forswear evangelism. Instead, we must strive through dialogue and all other means to help build a better and more just world. Pluralism is not an Asian concept. It has been suggested that an exclusive understanding of Christianity is really a form of religious imperialism of the western world towards other cultures. It is further suggested that Asian cultures are generally more tolerant, and perceive truth in more inclusive and conciliatory terms that favour a pluralistic theology of religions. However I would like to argue that the reality is nowhere as clear-cut.

Thus while there are inclusive elements in certain streams of Asian thought, it is incorrect to assert that Asian cultures are naturally all inclusive. Both Chinese/Korean Confucianism and Indian Hinduism (and for that matter, Buddhism and Islam also) have clear canons by which orthodoxy is defined and heterodoxy excluded. These have operated throughout China's and India's histories, and continue to do so today.

I suggest that the fundamental inspiration behind the present-day pressures towards inclusivism and pluralism in the theology of religions come from liberal western thought, living under the burden of the Enlightenment. The underlying assumption is that we know better today than the apostles and the New Testament writers, something which is accepted by most, if not all, pluralists. This is a product of Enlightenment thinking with its emphasis on rationality, belief in progress and humans as 'emancipated, autonomous individuals', and an optimistic faith in humanity in which 'new' always seems better.

This can only be sustained by ignoring the fact that the apostles worked in an environment which was certainly no less, if not more, pluralistic than today. Indeed, the pressures to conform and to accommodate, were all there in abundance during the first century of the Christian era. The charge that the apostles thought in exclusive terms because they belong to a 'classicist' culture is simply historically untenable. Apart from Jews and Christians, there were hardly any religious exclusivist at that time. If they were exclusive in their view of religions, which they were, it was certainly not learnt from the surrounding culture which was highly pluralistic.

Thus despite claims to the contrary, Asian cultures and religions are not necessarily theologically more inclusive than western Christianity – at best one may speak of relative tendencies. Yet even these must be stated with caution. The real problem, as we have noted, lies in Enlightenment thought which has created a 'plausibility structure' that relativizes everything, and which encourages doubt and pluralism to flourish. The conclusion should now be clear to us. Pluralism in its present-day form is primarily – though not exclusively – a liberal western problem, although its proponents have also drawn on inclusive elements in Asian thought in their attempts to universalise its appeal.

CONCLUDING COMMENTS

Firstly, pluralists have urged pluralism on others in the name of wanting to retreat from a past Christian imperialism. The earlier discussion on pluralism being in essence a liberal western agenda should alert us to the liberal tendency to view the whole world like itself. It appears that the real imperialism is being practiced today by those theologians who are using all the intellectual weaponry in their armoury to foist the new pluralist agenda on Christians, especially those in the two-thirds world.

The second comment is that many Asian writers in their zeal for the contextualisation of the Christian faith have, unfortunately, bought into the pluralist agenda, often as a means of affirming their 'Asianness'. If the arguments above are correct, then that is not only unnecessary, it is also wrong. True contextualisation, as we have already noted, must hold together in proper tension the indigenous and the pilgrim principles. That means the gospel must be rooted into Asian soil without losing its distinctiveness. A contextualisation that ends up in unfaithfulness to 'the faith that was once for all delivered to the saints' cannot claim to be a genuine incarnation of the gospel.

CHAPTER 5

ASIAN THEOLOGIES UP TO WORLD WAR TWO

World War Two is chosen as a convenient demarcation line for after that, the colonial period rapidly collapsed and newly independent churches began to emerge all over Asia. This spurred the search for more indigenous theologies in the post-war period. We will consider a selection.

MATTEO RICCI (1552-1610) AND
ACCOMMODATION TO A CHINESE CULTURE
Although Ricci was a western Jesuit missionary, his work, together with that of Robert de Nobili in India at the same time, occupy a pivotal place in the history of Asian Christianity. They were the first Christians to wrestle with the issues of contextualisation in the Asian context

Through faith and sheer doggedness, Ricci and his companion, Michele Ruggieri, entered China in 1583, and in 1600 they reached the imperial capital, Beijing. They began a work which, despite its ups and downs, led to the establishment of a permanent Catholic Church in China.

Aware of the Chinese distrust of foreigners, they adopted a cautious and discreet approach, mastering the Chinese language and the ancient classics. They dressed themselves like Chinese scholars to gain acceptability in high Chinese society. They called their preaching house *shuyuan* (academy) so as to present themselves as western men of learning, and not priests propagating a new religion. For as long as it was possible, Ricci consciously kept his true intentions hidden.

Ricci's work met with quick acceptance and response. Although it was probably their scientific and other skills that initially attracted the Chinese to them, in the end it was the moral and intellectual answers that led them to faith. In Christianity they found a moral discipline based upon an external, universal source which fortified the traditional values which were being eroded.

How are the efforts of Ricci and his colleagues to be measured according to the criteria of a mission-based theology? It is clear that the Jesuits were pioneering contextualisation in seventeenth century China. In the externals of dress, language and mastery of the classics, mannerisms and moral conduct, they identified successfully with Chinese society and culture. Further, in their use of mathematical and scientific knowledge, as a way to find a hearing for their message, they were addressing a demonstrable need in the minds of the Chinese, whose culture has always prized learning.

In their translations and writings, they were not afraid to relate traditional Christian concepts to indigenous Chinese terms, with all the associated risks involved. The best example concerns the choice of the term for God. Like the Apostle John had done in his use of the Greek *Logos*, they chose words which could form bridges for the communication of the gospel to other cultures. The Jesuits had decided in 1583 to use the term *Tianzhu* (Master of Heaven), although this was not native to the Chinese. They therefore borrowed the terms *Shangdi* (Sovereign on High) and *Tian* (Heaven) from the classics, and used them as equivalents to *Tianzhu*. In order to do so, they had to attribute theistic significance to *Shangdi* and *Tian*, a procedure that went against the whole Confucian tradition, which had always regarded them as a naturalistic anonymous power of order and animation in the universe.

It could be argued that Ricci went too far in his accommodation when he suggested that the rites in honour of ancestors and Confucius had no more than a civil significance, and were therefore permissible for the Christian. Such a distinction is not held within the Chinese worldview.

CONTENDING FOR THE FAITH:
THE BEGINNINGS OF INDIGENOUS CHINESE THEOLOGY
The beginning of the twentieth century brought difficult days for a once proud Chinese nation, which was in a state of serious decline due to a tired traditionalism and a blind refusal to come to terms with the modern world. In the hope of finding national salvation, it opened itself to foreign influences, including Christianity, as never before. However, 20 years later the attitude towards Christianity turned sour once again and the anti-Christian movement picked up steam from the 1920s onwards,

The Chinese church was unprepared for the onslaught, mainly because the form of Christianity that the missionaries brought was inadequate to meet these challenges. Faced with a people with an ancient and proud culture, who were now searching for a more adequate basis for it, the missionaries tended to be insensitive. To a politically and economically oppressed nation struggling to establish its national identity and integrity, the missionaries brought a gospel heavily tainted by the guilt of its imperialistic associations, both past and present. To a culture which invariably thought and functioned in holistic terms without any clear separation between theory and practice, spirit and matter, the gospel came in the form of a western dualism which promised salvation for the soul but not for the nation. And finally, to a people struggling to catch up with the oppressing western powers in science and technology, the gospel was presented in terms which were perceived as irrational and superstitious because it lacked an adequate apologetic.

To the credit of the Chinese church leaders, they responded quickly to the three-fold challenge of science and the modern world, of culture, and of nationalism and nation-building. The result was a Christocentric apologetic which focused on the character, supernatural acts (sometimes defended and sometimes jettisoned, depending on the theological leanings of the particular writer), mission and teachings of Jesus which accentuated his ethical appeal and social relevance. The return to the gospel of Jesus seemed to be the best ideological device to de-westernise the Christian message brought by the missionaries.

The challenge posed by culture was met by early efforts at the indigenisation of Chinese theology. The indigenous church is 'one which conserves and unifies all truths contained in both the Christian religion and in China's ancient civilisation and which thus manifests and expresses the religious life and experiences of the Chinese Christians in a fashion that is native and natural to them'.[12] The challenge was met by Christian writings addressing issues posed by both the Nationalists and the Communists.

The work of these thinkers in the 1920s reminds us of early Christian apologists like Justin Martyr and Tertullian, whose theologies were forged in the furnace of persecution and the anti-Christian attacks of their day. The Chinese writers made genuine efforts to develop a theology that sought to address the socio-political and cultural issues of the day. The whole exercise was designed to commend the gospel to the non-Christian Chinese and, therefore, took seriously both the apologetic and evangelistic concern of the church and faithfulness to the Christian tradition.

While they did their best, their opponents were in no mood to listen. It may well have been that their immediate achievements did not amount to much, but it appears that they had laid the foundations for what may eventually develop into a mature indigenous Chinese Christian theology. This appears to be suggested by the mainland Chinese scholar Wang Wei-fan (1990) in his review of how theological reflection has developed in China in the past 70 years, leading to a unity of faith, knowledge and action, and to a holistic theology. Wang also highlights the 'Christ-centeredness which has helped the church, in the post-war years, to overcome the divisions caused by fundamentalism modernism, and denominationalism, and to allow it to develop a theology that is more truly indigenous. If what Wang says is correct, then the work of the first generation of Chinese apologists has not been in vain!

NEHEMIAH GOREH (1825-95) AND THE RATIONAL REFUTATION OF HINDUISM

Nehemiah Goreh came from a Brahmin family and grew up deeply versed in Sanskrit and the Hindu tradition. His contact with the gospel came through evangelical Anglican missionaries but initially led to his determination to use his intellect to destroy it. Then followed a prolonged intellectual struggle before his conversion and baptism in 1848. Later in his life, he moved from evangelical Anglicanism to Anglo-Catholicism, and of all Indian Christians he was probably one of the most well-versed in the Hindu traditions.

Although he wrote a number of books, *A Rational Refutation of the Hindu Philosophical Systems* is the most significant. It was first published in Hindi in 1860 and then translated into English in 1862. It was a conscious rational apologetic effort, based on a close analysis of the Hindu texts, directed at the six traditional systems of Hindu philosophy, with about half of it devoted to the *Advaita Vedanta* (non-dualism) system.

Vedantic philosophy puts forward three levels of existence: true existence for *Brahman* (ultimate reality) alone; practical existence for the world, human souls and, *Isvara* the personal God; and illusory existence. To illustrate this, consider, for example, a rope which a man sees from afar and thinks is a snake. However, when he comes nearer he sees that it is really a rope. The snake has only illusory existence, the rope has practical existence. Yet the true Vedantin would say that only *Brahman* is real and therefore the rope remains illusory.

Thus according to the Vedantic position, the whole phenomenal world and God are ultimately unreal. Only when one sees beyond them to *Brahman*, does one sees true reality. The world's existence is not its own but *Brahman*'s. However, to Goreh, this cosmic illusionism is not a solution either. Goreh was concerned to show that the Vedantic philosophy based on *maya* (illusion) was riddled with incoherence. The strength of Goreh's apologetic has become more evident in light of present-day discussions.

There can be little doubt that Goreh's apologetic approach is soundly missiological. While he does not appear to have dealt much with socio-political issues, he was definitely concerned with the evangelistic thrust of the Indian church, especially to the higher castes. His rational approach employed logical arguments which were not foreign to Brahmin minds schooled in Hindu philosophy. The validity of his approach was demonstrated by the conversion of one of the most famous women from Hinduism, Pandita Ramabai, who like himself was highly skilled in Hindu philosophy and Sanskrit.

Goreh's writings have been rightly compared with the theology of the early church, developed out of the writings of people like the Alexandrian Fathers, and shaped by pastoral and apologetic concerns. Partly because of this recognition, there appears to be a revival of interest in his work in recent years.

SADHU SUNDAR SINGH (1889-1929):
THE WATER OF LIFE IN AN INDIAN CUP
Sundar Singh has been described as the most famous Indian Christian who ever lived, and no Indian Christian has exercised an influence remotely comparable. Yet, strangely, there appears to be

relatively little discussion on him in recent Indian theological writings.

Sundar Singh was born a Sikh and, under the strong influence of his mother, was brought up in both the Sikh and the Hindu *bhakti* traditions. In December 1904, after his mother had died, he became a Christian following a traumatic spiritual experience which included a vision of the Risen Christ in the middle of the night. He was baptised, and at the age of sixteen, in fulfilment of his mother's hopes, donned the ochre robe to become a *sadhu*. This term in India refers to a holy man who is devoted to a life of simplicity – although for Sundar Singh, this was as a Christian. He entered an Anglican seminary in 1909 but left after less than a year to begin an evangelistic preaching ministry that took him, first, throughout India and to Tibet and ultimately, all over the world.

Apart from his commitment to evangelism, the other distinctive aspect of his life was his understanding of the spiritual realm. This was what both captivated his western audiences in his later ministry, and also created all sorts of problems for them. For example, in his prayer life he sought a constant communion with God. He laid claim to visions and slipped in and out of (what Hindu India calls) *Samadhi*, 'altered states of consciousness'. Yet he was always careful to test everything, including his visions, by scripture. Miracles and healings apparently were the norm in his ministry, as attested by his own writings and those of his biographers. He worked within, and addressed the concerns of, the worldview of those among whom he ministered, his methods firmly rooted in his own culture. He constantly used parables drawn from everyday life in India and regularly employed a recognised Indian pattern of reasoning, which dealt with issues, not by precise logic, but by use of a vivid analogy which illumined the subject. By living as a *sadhu* and a *sannyasi*, he used a contextual model of preaching and teaching with which Indians were familiar and readily accepted.

Theologically he was orthodox and he would have rejected the pluralist position. He saw Christianity as a fulfilment of India's religious quest, seeing the 'Logos' at work everywhere, even in non-Christian cultures and scriptures, preparing for the full revelation of Christ in the gospel. Hinduism and Buddhism may have dug the canals, but they have no living water with which to fill them. 'Christ is the water to flow through these channels.' He was deeply convinced that his people needed Christ, the 'Water of Life', but he was equally adamant that 'they do not want it in European vessels but in an Indian cup'.

BRAHMABANDHAB UPADHYAYA (1861-1907): BEYOND THE 'LATIN CAPTIVITY' OF THE INDIAN CHURCH

Brahmabandhab Upadhyaya felt that the best way to present the Christian faith to India's thinkers was to use Vedantic categories. For him, 'Indian thought can be made just as useful to Christianity as Greek thought has been to Europe. The truths of the Hindu philosopher must be used as stepping-stones to the Catholic Faith.' It was not just a matter of drawing interesting parallels between Christianity and Hinduism. Rather, having come to know God in Christ, he found that the Vedantic teachings were fulfilled more profoundly in Christ than Sankara the eighth century Hindu philosopher.

Probably the best way to capture Brahmabandhab's attempt to communicate contextually is to quote his hymn on the Trinity as *Saccidananda* (the ultimate unchanging reality) written originally in Sanskrit:

I bow to Him who is Being (*Sat*), Consciousness (*Chit*) and Bliss (*Ananda*),

I bow to Him whom world minds loathe,
Whom pure minds yearn for, the Supreme Abode.

He is the Supreme, the Ancient of days, the Transcendent,
Indivisible Plenitude, Immanent yet above all things,
Three-fold relation, pure, unrelated, knowledge beyond knowledge.

The Father, Sun, Supreme Lord, unborn,
The Seedless Seed of the tree of becoming,
The Cause of all, Creator, Providence, Lord of the universe.

The infinite and perfect Word,
The Supreme Person begotten,
Sharing in the Father's nature, Conscious by essence, Giver of true Salvation.

He who proceeds from Being and Consciousness,
Replete with the breath of perfect bliss,
The Purifier, the Swift, the Revealer of the Word, the Life-giver.

Here we see the language of India blended creatively and beautifully with those from Scriptural and Greek sources to present powerfully the Christian understanding of God to the Hindu mind.

There can be little doubt that this is the right direction for theology in India. There are a number of good reasons for using *Brahman* for God in the Hindu context, and the charge that it is too Hindu a concept is no more serious than the one that the terms *Logos, ousia, hypostasis,* are too Stoic or Platonic.

However, we must not forget the 'Pilgrim Principle' of Walls and risk. losing our Christian distinctiveness in the contextualisation process. Ultimately, is the essence of this *Brahman* defined by Biblical or Vedantic categories? Unfortunately, the answers given by the Indian church has been ambiguous. Unless this is resolved, the Indian church may end up misleading the worldwide church in the pluralism debate, just as Arius did in the Christological controversy centuries ago in the relationship between God the Father and God the Son.

TOYOHIKO KAGAWA (1888-1960):
HOLISTIC EVANGELISM AND PROPHETIC SOCIAL WITNESS

Toyohiko Kagawa was one of the most well-known Japanese Christians whose father was well-to-do and whose mother was a concubine. His parents died when he was young and after his Christian conversion he was disinherited by his uncle. He trained in the Presbyterian College, Tokyo, and Kobe Theological Seminary, and then from 1915-1917 at Princeton, USA. Having seen the appalling physical and moral conditions of the Kobe slums, and convinced that the people there would not listen to the gospel from an outsider, in 1909 he moved into a squalid cubicle six feet square. From there he began a ministry of evangelism and social outreach that has captured the imagination of the Christian world ever since.

Much of the plight and poverty of the slum was caused by the effect of industrialisation on the nation. As a Christian socialist, he cared for the sick and destitute, working at unionising both industrial workers and peasants at a time when that was illegal, rescuing women from vice and setting up co-operatives. He shunned violence and opposed Japanese military aggression overseas. For his efforts, he was often in trouble with the police and sometimes imprisoned. His work contributed to the efforts that provoked the government in the mid-1920s to wipe out slums in the major cities and legalise labour unions. Public recognition gradually came his way. In the 1930s he was made the chief advisor to Tokyo's welfare bureau at the height of the depression. After the war he also served for a period as special adviser to the government on public welfare.

Kagawa was also an indefatigable evangelist. With a burning passion 'to make Christ known' he started the Kingdom of God Movement in Japan which brought together two-thirds of the Protestant churches from 1929-1932. He once expressed his goal as 'the salvation of 100,000 poor, hasten the day of the emancipation of 9,430,000 labourers toiling in various fields and liberate 20,000,000 tenant farmers'.

Easily misunderstood, his theological beliefs put him in the fundamentalist camp of his time, although he held the optimistic view that post-conversion humanity is capable of an absolute ethic of love through which the Kingdom of God can be realised. This places him in the social gospel camp.

Kagawa wrote more than 60 books in his life-time, with some two million copies sold, covering a diverse range of topics. Like John Wesley, one of his mentors, he also combined holistic evangelism with prophetic social witness, and both remain relevant today.

CONCLUDING REMARKS

From these examples, it is clear that there have been some highly commendable efforts made in setting theology within an Asian context. All the above writers and thinkers were, in different ways, passionately concerned with the mission of the church, the effect of the gospel to make an impact on the society in which they lived, to evangelise and build Christian lives, to grow the church, or to speak theologically in indigenous terms.

Each had their limitations. Ricci and his friends in the seventeenth century were clearly over-accommodating in the matter of ancestral rites. Brahmabandhab Upadhyaya and other Indian theologians who wanted to speak of the Trinity in terms of

Brahman as *Saccidananda*, have yet to convince the wider Christian world that they have been as careful in their definition of terms as John the Apostle was in his of *Logos*. Sundar Singh, owing to Franciscan influence, had little time for the burning socio-political issues of his day. Kagawa's worldview was almost certainly too secularised for him to be the best evangelist to Japan.

However, these weaknesses do not lessen their achievements, or nullify their ideal of making the gospel relevant to the context in which they were working, and subsequently post-World War Two writers have been able to build on the labours of these pioneers.

CHAPTER 6
ECUMENICAL ASIAN THEOLOGIES AFTER WORLD WAR TWO

In the last chapter we examined how the criteria which we had earlier delineated for a missiological or contextual theology was illustrated in different ways by examples of Asian theology articulated before World War Two. These criteria are relevant in the first instance to socio-political concerns; second to the efficacy of the church's evangelistic and pastoral concerns; thirdly, to inculturation; and, fourthly to faithfulness to the Christian tradition.

In this and the next chapter we will apply these four criteria to some Protestant theological writings in the post-war Two period to assess their adequacy or otherwise as contextual theologies. We will begin in this chapter by looking at theologies from ecumenical circles. These include the work of four individuals who have been widely associated with the ecumenical movement in different ways.

D. T. NILES (1908-1970):
ECUMENISM WITH EVANGELISM
Daniel Thambyrajah Niles studied at the United Theological College at Bangalore and began a ministry in both the Methodist Church and the ecumenical movement that led to his becoming one of the most well known international figures over four decades in Ceylon (Sri Lanka). At the time of his death, he was a President of the World Council of Churches and President of the Methodist Church in Sri Lanka.

The formative theological influences of his life came from the evangelical piety of his Methodist heritage. His great-grandfather was the first Tamil baptised by the American Board Mission, and his grandfather was a Methodist pastor. He never pretended to be a great theologian but is remembered as a great preacher, evangelist and pastor.

The primary concern of his theology was evangelism, which he defined in a most memorable Asian manner: 'It is one beggar telling another beggar where to get food. It is not a program, it is being a Christian and relating the gospel to the torments of the world.'

In this task of evangelism, the church is central in preparing for the coming of the kingdom and the objective of the missionary enterprise is to plant and build up of indigenous churches in every land. The church is not only God's instrument of the gospel but part of the gospel itself, which must have a clear sense of self-identity in order to fulfil its role in God's purposes. However, he was also concerned that in the church's search for self-identity, the stone of stumbling must never be removed to make the gospel more acceptable. His abhorrence of denominationalism with all its restrictive structures obstructing the mission and life of the younger churches at every point is illustrated by his story of the Japanese immigration officer who inquired about a missionary's faith: 'Yes, Madam, Christian – but what damnation?'

Hinduism 'saves' by removing humans from this world. Thus, 'The Hindu needs no doctrine of redemption within history', whereas, 'The Christian is lost without it'. Christian salvation is, 'not simply salvation of the soul. It is the salvation of the whole man and of the whole universe and human history'.'

Nevertheless, it has been noted that Niles says 'very little about specific social and political applications of the gospel',[13] for Niles' stance is that he saw himself first and foremost as an evangelist and preacher – his commitment to evangelism is unquestionable.

In his critique of the 'westernity' of Christianity, Niles argues that there remains 'the task of addressing eastern cultures with a relevant and a pungent theology, making the church in eastern lands congruous with its background'. He wrestled seriously in his evangelism with peoples of other faiths and his approach to this was not that of the ruthless rational apologetic, but of a more gentle evangelistic dialogue between friends, walking alongside each other.

His theology was largely written in a more practical way, with sermons and bible studies, rather than in purely academic studies. One of his greatest contributions to the indigenisation of worship in Asia was his work on the *EACC Hymnal* (1963), wherein the wealth of the Asian church is gathered together, probably for the first time on such a scale. Niles wrote the words of some 45 of the translated hymns, giving to them fresh power and beauty in the English language.

In terms of the present-day issue of pluralism, he was absolutely clear in his affirmation of Christ's uniqueness. 'Christ must be exalted Lord, because of all teachers and founders of religions he is the greatest, the noblest, the only sinless and true.' Elsewhere he wrote, '...there is no other name given by which men can be saved except the name of Jesus Christ '.

If Niles is unambiguous on religious pluralism, he is less so on eternal salvation, rejecting the absolutist position which asserts that those who have the opportunity to own Christ, but turn him down, will be eternally lost. He argues that this does not represent the total thrust of New Testament teaching. Indeed, he tries to hold together the tensions in the following manner: 'Salvation is indeed God's possibility, but it also remains man's responsibility ... With God all things are possible, but for man damnation remains a possibility also.'

However, the more important question that must be asked of Niles is that, given his 'soft' universalistic position, does not that in some serious manner detract us from the rationale for preaching the gospel which he so passionately affirms? Is there not a severe tension in his theology which cannot be held together for long without something or other giving way?

Niles wished to maintain a reverent agnosticism about the question of the eternal destiny of each person, a position which I believe properly represents New Testament theology. Yet could not this have been combined with the equally valid New Testament affirmation that those who persistently reject the truth will not be saved, and that this will indeed be the destiny of some, thus lessening some of the severe (and unnecessary) tensions in his theology?

To sum up, Niles' theology is missiologically strong on the evangelistic and pastoral tasks of the church, but at best fair in relation to the socio-political context. Apart from the neglect of the 'excluded middle', he would be rated strong in his efforts to embody Christianity into the cultural idiom of Asia. Theologically he is strongly orthodox, except for his views on universal salvation.

MADATHIPARAMPIL MAMMEN THOMAS (1916-1996)
AND A CHRISTIAN *KARMA MARGA*

MM Thomas came from Kerala in south India and was nurtured in the 'evangelical and sacramental piety' of the Mar Thoma Church. Graduating from college at 19, he worked in both secular and Christian jobs. He read widely and came into contact with Gandhism and Marxism and was rejected as a candidate for ordination because he was too Marxist, and by the Communist Party for membership because he was a Christian!

He had many appointments culminating in his appointment as Chairman of the Central Committee of the World Council of Churches (1968-75). His contributions in all these areas were recognised by the award of the 1966 Luce Professorship at Union Theological Seminary, New York, and honorary doctorates by Serampore, Leiden and Uppsala. Without formal theological training (except for one brief year in 1953 at Union), he became 'Asia's foremost lay theologian'.[14]

For him, theology was always a living and contextual theology, grappling with human problems in the midst of the socio-political and scientific-technological realities of the day.

Shaped though dialogue with secular ideologies and other renascent religions, he affirmed that the gospel is 'the foundation of a true secular humanism'. He argued that the Christian hope should not be presented as an alternative to the human hopes and aspirations of secular humanist utopias, but the gospel of Christ should be presented as the power which can redeem revolutionary Asia from its 'most terrible perversions' and re-establish it in such a way that it does not betray, but realise, its true human ends.

Thomas takes the same approach towards the religions of Asia, especially renascent Hinduism, which he sees as acting as a powerful force for social reform in India. He illustrates this in *The Acknowledged Christ of the Indian Renaissance* (1969). Here he surveys how the thinking of some of the foremost spiritual leaders of modern India, especially in neo-Hinduism, including Radhakrishnan and Gandhi, have been influenced by Christ's teachings. Ultimately, the Christian faith transcends all ideologies and religions, but through dialogue the Christian seeks to evaluate and renew them, and thus the gospel becomes the basis of a genuine humanism whereby the world is transformed and a new humanity emerges.

Against the background of the church's disillusionment and suspicions of all human ideologies and utopias, Thomas has been peerless in his advocacy of Christian social engagement and involvement in nation-building among Asian Christians of his generation.

While he does affirm the validity of evangelism in his writings, it appears peripheral to his thinking. As far as inculturation goes, his 'living theology' implies a holistic perspective and a rejection of the separation between truth and practice. At the same time, he is averse to any attempts at inculturation if, 'it is merely exploited for the conversion of individuals and the numerical growth of the Church'. He does not deal with the healing or exorcism ministries, but interprets the 'principalities and powers' in essentially sociological and ideological, rather than spiritual, terms. Here Thomas reveals the extent of the secularisation and westernisation of his worldview.

Thomas's definition of the gospel is confusing at best. For him the 'irreducible core' is the 'faith acknowledgement of the centrality of the Person of Jesus Christ for the individual and social life of mankind', but this always takes different forms and shapes in different historical contexts. Such a minimalist definition of the gospel is highly problematic, and it is clear that there is a fundamental ambiguity in his definition of what is the irreducible core of the Christian faith.

In terms of the identity of the church, Thomas' starting point is that New Testament *koinonia* does not refer primarily to the church or the quality of life within the church, but that it is the manifestation of the new reality of the kingdom at work in the world of men in world history. Thus, 'the new humanity in Christ… which responds in faith and receives the liberation of Jesus Christ as Lord and Savior, transcends the Church'. God's saving purpose is not limited to the church – that is, the visible church. His liberating faith and grace should, therefore, be discernible outside it. The church must learn to recognise, 'a form of the Church (partial no doubt) in the Christ-centred fellowship of faith emerging outside the Church'.

This has been strongly criticised by, among others, Lesslie Newbigin. First, Newbigin argues that Thomas' understanding of *koinonia* is highly mistaken. None of the 18 references to that word in the New Testament allows for the interpretation Thomas gives to it. Indeed, one of them, 2 Cor 6:14, specifically denies that there can be *koinonia* between believers and unbelievers. Thomas wants a gospel without any 'stones of stumbling'. It is clear that Thomas' ambiguity about the 'irreducible core' of the Christian faith leads him into a fuzzy ecclesiology.

To sum up, it goes without saying that Thomas' clarion call to the church for socio-political engagement is strong and cannot be faulted. This will probably be his most lasting contribution to twentieth century Asian Christian thought. However, his understanding of how to set the gospel within its Asian context tends to be limited to its relation with socio-political issues and to the dialogue with indigenous religions. Most problematic of all is his understanding of what constitutes the 'irreducible core' of the Christian faith and the church in the context of a religiously pluralistic world. His ecclesiology tends towards a spiritual and disembodied conception of the Christian message. For Thomas the Christian gospel, like the Cheshire cat in Alice in Wonderland, is there without a trace of the institution – without Christianity, without Christ, without Bible – just the disembodied grin.

KOSUKE KOYAMA (1929-2009) AND 'WATER BUFFALO' THEOLOGY

Kosuke Koyama was born in a Christian home in Tokyo. There he lived through the war years and witnessed the devastation brought by American bombs in response to the 'idolatry' and 'greed' of Meiji Japan. Graduating from Tokyo Union Theological Seminary in 1952, he served for a while as a minister of the United Church of Christ in Japan, before furthering his studies at Drew University and Princeton Theological Seminary in United States. Subsequently he taught at the Thailand Theological Seminary (1960-8), was Director of the Association of Theological Schools in South-East Asia (1968-74), lectured at the University of Otago, New Zealand, and after 1980 taught at Union Theological Seminary, New York.

His writings often dazzle by their vivid imageries borrowed from everyday life and human history, ranging from frogs croaking in the Thai monsoon rains, to modern technology wherein a *Three*

Mile an Hour God may be more efficient than a jumbo-jet. He detests theology written in an academic style where the authors do their best 'to discourage people from reading them'.

Second, his interpretation of Biblical texts is people-centred and contextual. In his best known book, *Water Buffalo Theology*, he speaks of how he came to realise in his work in Thailand that what really matters is not a set of doctrines called Buddhism, but *people* who are trying to live according to the doctrine of Buddha, and he found the study of the Buddh*ists* far more interesting and exciting than Buddh*ism*. For him the test of any theology in a given situation lies in its ability to address the concerns of the listener. Thus all theology has to be subordinated, in his particular case, to the needs of the 'cock-fighting' farmers of Thailand.

The theological centre in Koyama's thought is the *theologia crucis* of Luther, on whom he wrote his doctoral dissertation. The 'broken Christ' who 'heals the world broken by idolatry'.

Throughout his writings there is the constant interaction with many issues in the light of the Cross of Christ. These include imperialism, both past and present, idolatry of power and wealth in national and international affairs, problems faced by racial, economic and religious minorities, and ecology. He is more reflective than Thomas, but both standpoints are necessary. 'Ideology without theology – that leaves little room for hope; theology without ideology – that leaves little scope for action'.[15] In one of his clearest statements on evangelism, he writes:

> *Christianity is so self-righteous that I do not see much future for it. It wants to teach. It does not want to learn … It is suffering from a 'teaching complex' … People have become the object of evangelism since it is understood by Christians that people are 'automatically' living in the darkness, untrustworthy, wicked, adulterous and unsaved … The 'teacher complex' expresses itself in a 'crusade complex' … Christian faith does not and cannot be spread by crusading. It will spread without money, without bishops, without theologians, without plannings, if people see a crucified mind, not a crusading mind, in Christians.[16]*

In Christian evangelism and missions, the west has been the centre for four centuries, but their centre-based theologies (of the 'blond Jesus') have had more than 100 years of painful irrelevance to the world outside of the west. Again, in response to the claim of a western missiologist that 'the first stirrings of the new life' were given by the gospel to millions in Asia, Koyama counters by saying that, 'Eastern civilisation has refused to become Christian.' Moreover he asks, 'Do "the first stirrings of the new life" come from missiology of *theologia crucis* or from the rage of the western psyche?'

Koyama is saying things that the church needs to hear more often, but at the same time, he overstates his case. After all, his own grandfather became a Christian through a Cambridge graduate who could speak of the lordship of Jesus without running down Buddhism or Japanese culture! While it may be true that there are relatively few Christians in Japan and India, this does not apply to Singapore, Taiwan, Indonesia, South Korea and, possibly, even China – not to mention Philippines.

It appears that Koyama is deeply burdened by the 'western guilt complex' in missions. What comes across so powerfully in Koyama's writings is the Christian's need to put on 'the crucified mind'. But when this plea is adulterated by a distorted 'western guilt complex', he ends up being almost apologetic about the proclamation of the gospel. One needs to ask if this hesitation comes from a missiology of *theologia crucis*, or from the unresolved conscience of the *Japanese* psyche, burdened by a national history no less imperialistic than the west in the first half of the twentieth century?

Koyama shows little or no awareness of the healing and exorcism ministry of the church. Of course he speaks about the world of spirits in Asian thought, but only as images. At every point his interpretation of anything related to this realm is secularised.

In terms of faithfulness to the Christian tradition, Koyama interacts constantly with the message of the Bible in his writings. If he uses borrowed Buddhist vocabulary to communicate the gospel, he nevertheless seeks to give to it biblical meaning. He has always pleaded for a more positive attitude towards other religions against the background of the generally negative view taken earlier by western Christianity. Thus he argues that we should avoid speaking of the superiority of Christianity (as opposed to Christ) as a religion over other religions. It is not a problem to affirm that which is good and true in other religions. Rather, only if we insist that the salvation in Buddha and Jesus Christ are identical, then we misrepresent the gospel.

Koyama's theology displays a strong sensitivity to the socio-political context of Asia, but it is positively weak on the evangelistic and pastoral dimensions. He takes inculturation seriously, although his neglect of the 'excluded middle' reveals his captivity to the western secularised worldview. Finally, his apparent indifference to doctrines and implicit religious pluralism raises serious questions about his faithfulness to the apostolic faith.

C. S. SONG (1929-) AND THE THEOLOGY OF TRANSPOSITION

Song comes from the Presbyterian Church of Taiwan and is today's most well known Chinese theologian. He studied in Taiwan University, and then in New College, Edinburgh and Union Theological Seminary, New York. He was the Principal of Tainan Theological College (1965-70), and served with the Reformed Church of America (1971-73) and, thereafter, as the Associate Director, Commission on Faith and Order, World Council of Churches. Since 1985, he has been teaching at the Pacific School of Religion, California. Of all Asian theologians today, Song is probably the most widely published.

He rejects any emphasis on mission which focuses on conversion into a Christianity distorted, as he perceives it, by western-centric hermeneutics. Instead he argues for a secularised and political interpretation of mission by a Christianity which has been universalised by a doctrine of God working redemptively in all human history. While Song takes the significance of Christ seriously, nowhere in his writings is a clear set of criteria given which helps us understand how he discerns the reality of Christ in the Asian experience.

He takes both the Bible and Asian cultures and religions with equal seriousness, but offers no clear criteria for discerning Christ's presence in the latter. Thus he appears to have turned the Christian message into something different from classical Christianity, as opposed to western Christianity.

As part of his protest against the westernisation of the gospel, he dislikes dogma, but a problem arises when he makes no distinction between the dogmas of western denominationalism and the core of the apostolic faith that has been handed down through the centuries to the present.

Furthermore, there is a strident universalism not found in classical Christianity running through his writings. Universalism is to be preferred over conditional immortality because it is more consistent with the final hope that all things will find their fullness in God. There is a passionate concern for the salvation of Asian humanity, which is what lies behind his refusal to allow the salvation history in the Bible a place of uniqueness.

This leads to the third and clearest indication of his departure from apostolic Christianity, his implicit pluralism. Song's fundamental starting point is that the claim of uniqueness in Biblical salvation history is a western imposition on the Christian faith. He prefers to regard it as a pattern or a type of God's salvation, manifested in a concentrated way in ancient Israel and in the history of the church, and therefore to be discovered in varied degrees in other nations and peoples.. This implicit pluralism is relentlessly pursued in all his writings. Consequently, 'Life without Immanuel is an illusion, but life is God-is-with-us and that is why in Asia we have Gautama Buddha, Mo Ti, Shinran and Gandhi.'

The reference to Gandhi is particularly telling. Despite his explicit rejection of the unique divinity of Christ and his atonement for sinful humanity, nevertheless for Song, Gandhi is 'a sign of God for us Christians also'. Nowhere does Song give us any criterion as to how to distinguish between that which is divine action and that which is not. Is Gandhi 'a sign of God for us' in his acceptance of Christ's 'Sermon on the Mount' as well as his rejection of Christ's divinity and atonement? If it is only the former, on what basis is that judgement made?

Song has in fact changed the gospel into something different. One of his basic criticisms of western Christian missions in Asia is their general failure to come to terms with the socio-political implications of the gospel in the Asian context. The consequence is that the Asian church 'completely fails to realise that Jesus Christ intended to bring about a radical change of social order through a radical change of individual men and women'. After all, conversion is not simply a personal affair but 'a social event contributing to the emergence of a new social order'. A critical prophetic note against the travesties of justice, equality and freedom in the Asian scene runs through all his writings.

If Song appears strong on the socio-political implications of the gospel, he is correspondingly weak on the evangelistic and pastoral dimensions. He has little sympathy with evangelism as winning people to Christ and church-planting, but rather it is politically defined. 'Evangelization is an act of empowering people to suffer unto hope',[17] and 'the church is an event',[18] which happens whenever God's work of redemption takes place, which is not meant to be identified with a permanent social organization brought into existence through the act of Christ.

Song's approach to reconstruct mission and Christian theology is at one with his agenda to de-westernise Asian Christianity. As he once put it in a public lecture, he does not want Asian Christians to have to sing 'a foreign song in the Lord's land'. His story-telling style is very typically Chinese.

However, here we come to a seeming paradox. A number of observers have commented that his theology is not really very Asian and that rather than being a plain reading of the Christian text from within the Asian soul, reads more like a western Enlightenment reading of the Bible, heavily coloured with Asian illustrations.

It may be even more than that. Having shorn his Christian faith of absolutes through the Enlightenment captivity of his thought, he appears to have had to look elsewhere for absolutes. What he appears to have done is to have replaced the classical Christian understanding of history with a Chinese reading of it. Thus, unlike Thomas and Koyama who challenge Hindu and Buddhist readings of history with the Christian view, Song reverses the process and jettisons the Christian view for the Chinese.

Despite Song's intentions, his approach actually militates against the very agenda of transposition that he is so concerned with. Song, with his insistence that God the Redeemer is found in the histories of all cultures, has effectively removed all need for transposition. If God's truth is equally found in one context already, what need is there for it to be transposed from another context? Thus it is not without justification that HD Beeby writes, in an unpublished poem, 'On Recent Writings by CS Song':

Oh dear, what next?
The Context has now
Become the text.
And I'm so afraid
The day will come…
And he stoutly maintains
Though it sounds absurd,
That now the flesh
Has become the Word. *(emphasis mine)*

As with Thomas and Koyama, there is no doubt that Song is inspired by a vision of Christ bringing dignity, equality and freedom to Asian societies. He also calls for an incarnational Christianity that affirms the value of Asian cultures and religions, which in the past have been treated disparagingly by much of western Christianity. However, his presuppositions have been so influenced by Enlightenment thinking, that his version of Christianity comes across as something different from the apostolic faith. Moreover, these very presuppositions contradict the very agenda of transposition that he so passionately advocates. This leads to a theology of mission which has little room for evangelism and pastoral concern.

Song is concerned that Asian societies will be marked by justice and freedom, dignity and respect for human rights, equality and economic well-being in the modern world. Few Asian Christians would disagree with this. What, however, appears to have been forgotten, is that the roots of such a humanitarian vision owe much to western civilisation's Christian origins. Admittedly, some of these ideas have also emerged in fragmented forms throughout history in various societies, but what is beyond doubt is that no other culture or society, in Asia and elsewhere, built upon a non-Christian basis has ever evolved the same comprehensive vision in and of itself. Its emergence in the modern world, undergirded by a strong legal framework which was developed to protect it from being compromised, presupposes the whole experience of the history of western Civilisation, which was strongly impacted and undeniably shaped by Christianity.

Yet Song and others, who are so inspired by the vision of justice and *shalom* in our world and write so passionately to inspire its birth, strenuously deny the relevance of evangelism, Christian conversion, and church-planting which lie at the basis of building such a Christian history for Asian societies. In the end, his project of de-westernisation of Christianity has not left the gospel any leverage to transform his own setting. In short, overall Song's theology must be adjudged as weak from a mission-based standpoint.

MINJUNG THEOLOGY AND POLITICAL LIBERATION IN KOREA

On May 16, 1961 a military coup took place in South Korea following which modernisation policies were introduced which led to a rapid growth of industrialisation and a corresponding increase in the gross national product. In the process, President Park's dictatorial regime exploited South Korea's only available resource in pursuit of its economic objectives, that of the relatively well-educated, industrious work force. This resulted in an overall economic deprivation of both rural peasants and urban workers characterised by low wages, long hours, and hazardous working conditions, as well as a widening gap between the rich and poor.

Against this dehumanising background, combined with Park's repressive political policies, many mainline churches remained relatively silent. However, some pastors and lay church workers set about creating urban and rural mission organisations aimed at alleviating the suffering of the poor. Increasingly, groups like the Korean Student Christian Federation and the Korean National Council of Churches started to protest openly. Around 1975 a small group of theologians began to develop the idea of a theology of the *minjung* as a contextual Korean theology.

Etymologically, the word *minjung* means 'the mass of the people'. Theologically, the *minjung* is present wherever there is socio-cultural alienation, economic exploitation and political suppression. In the Bible, these are the foreigners, the widows, the orphans, the poor and the 'sinners', and in the Korean setting they are the poor farmers, the exploited industrialised workers, the urban squatters and the beggars.

Minjung theology is the reflection of those theologians who have a guilt complex about themselves not being *minjung* trying to understand and learn from them, and through them trace the genuine message of the 'Jesus for sinners' behind the pages of the New Testament. They do this in relation to a theology of justice, love and freedom, addressing not so much the *minjung* themselves, but Christians and the public in general.

There are at least three biblical models for the theology of the *minjung*. The first is the exodus event. The second is the crucifixion and resurrection, a political event, since it is clear that Jesus was condemned and executed as a political offender. The third is Jesus' mission to those called sinners by the religious leaders of the time – the poor, the sick, the crippled, the tax-collectors, the widows, and the prostitutes. These are the *minjung*, which despite the changes across the centuries, still reflect the political and revolutionary nature of Jesus' true teachings. The historical and earthly aspirations of the *minjung* must act as a counterbalance to Christianity being seen solely as an other-worldly faith.

Through the study of the socio-economic history, literature and art forms, and the religious belief of the *minjung*, various movements can be discovered. Included among these are the Donghak revolution of the late nineteenth century against both feudal and foreign oppressions, and the 1960 Student Revolution inspired by democratic concerns. These three paradigms – from the Bible, church history, and *minjung* history – form the bases for the emerging theology.

Some of the methodological tools used by *minjung* theology involve re-interpreting models from the Bible, church history, and Korean history, as well as using the stories of the *minjung* to unmask the structures of oppression and the use of the traditional art forms of the Korean poor such as the mask dance .

There is no doubt that the *minjung* theologians are firmly on target. The indifference of the vast majority of the Korean churches to political repression and economic exploitation from the 1960s onwards has left them politically neutral or silent. *Minjung* theology's concern for socio-political transformation poses a fundamental challenge to Korean Christianity today.

There is, however, a corresponding weakness in its evangelistic and pastoral concerns. To begin with, nowhere in its writings are the issues of evangelism and pastoral nurture in the church taken seriously.

Furthermore, in terms of inculturation, *minjung* theology employs methods that are indigenous to Korea in its use of folk stories and the mask dance to understand the concerns and perceptions of the *minjung*, and to also communicate them. Again, it transcends the dualism inherent in much of the western theology, particularly in its reinterpretation of Korean church history.

One good example is found in the translation of the Bible into the Korean vernacular script used by the common people. It led to the injection of Christian language and its liberating message into the language of the poor. This was one reason why the ordinary Korean responded so favourably to a western religion. In another example, Korea's Confucian background does not allow Korean Christianity to separate the individual from society. Thus when the Korean Christians prayed, their prayer to God was, 'save my country and save my soul'. Even the dualistic filters of the missionaries' Christianity could not stop the Koreans, with their holistic worldview, from correctly reading the Bible.

Yet in other ways, *minjung* theology fails to take inculturation seriously. To begin with, although it rejects western dualism at one level, it accepts it at another through its adoption of a secularised worldview. For example, stories in the gospels on deliverance from demon-possession are conditioned by the socio-political oppression of the day. Political persecution by a foreign nation is said to be the hot-bed for producing deranged persons.

Thus, on the one hand, *minjung* theology has rightly rejected a western dualistic interpretation of the gospel which only applies it to the spiritual and religious dimensions. Yet on the other, in its secularised interpretations of shamanism and the spirit world, it shows that it has bought right into the same dualistic premises, except that it has erred in a direction exactly opposite to the one it criticises. Whereas earlier western missionaries may have been guilty of spiritualising the gospel, *minjung* writers have secularised both the gospel and the world. Furthermore, despite its assertion that it is a Korean theology, it is heavily influenced by non-Korean theologies. These influences include, among others, theologies of secularisation, of politics, of liberation, of *missio dei* and especially of laughter, play and festivity.

In terms of faithfulness to the Christian tradition, perhaps it is best to begin with a critical examination of the concept of *han* which is *minjung* theology's attempted reinterpretation of the doctrine of sin. In Korean this can be translated as 'just indignation' and 'a deep feeling that rises out of the unjust experience of the people'.

Theologically, it is the opposite of the traditional Christian idea of sin. Sin is our wrongdoing against God and our neighbours; *han* is the suffering of the 'sinned-against'. Sin is the unjust action of the oppressor, *han* is the passive pain suffered by the oppressed.

Further, *han* is an underlying feeling of the Korean people. Some psychoanalysts see this as the psychosomatic sickness of most Koreans. This sickness arises out of the feeling of injustice, defeat, resignation and nothingness, which can be cured only when the structure and culture of the oppressed society is changed. At the same time, it is a tenacity for life which empowers the weak. Thus it can sometimes be channelled to great artistic expressions, or erupt as the energy for a revolution or rebellion through which the social and cultural structures of oppression are changed, the *han* of the *minjung* is resolved, and their sickness cured.

In the exposition of *han*, the impression is clearly given that the *minjung* cannot be attributed with sin at all, or even if they are, 'Jesus never rebukes these'. This excessive optimism about human nature effectively rejects the traditional Christian understanding of sin, which is rooted in humanity's radical alienation from God and our consequent bondage to it and hence our need for divine redemption. Sin is reduced to a merely socio-political entity, attributable only to the oppressor and never to the oppressed *minjung*. The gospel of the forgiveness of sin through the cross is replaced by a concern for the 'resolution of *han*' of the *minjung*, which comes about in two ways. On the victim's side, through psychological self-awakening *han* is recognised and, eventually, transcendence over it is attained. On the oppressor's side, socio-political action is necessary to remove the *han*-causing elements. Thus, at best *minjung* theology's concept of *han* leads to a one-sided secularised interpretation of the Christian concept of sin, built upon a dualistic worldview.

In terms of a genuinely missiological theology, *minjung* theology is strong on its socio-political emphasis, but correspondingly very weak in evangelistic and pastoral concerns. It may be rated as fair with respect to inculturation. As to its claim to faithfulness to the Christian tradition, it seems that at the very least a serious case can be made against it.

Thus *minjung* theology is a serious attempt by some concerned Korean theologians to respond to the Korean context of the 1960s and thereafter. Its advocates appear to have been so strongly influenced by post-Enlightenment western thought and theology that its claim to be Korean is rather ambivalent. It actually looks more like a theology shaped by various liberal versions of western political, liberation and secular theologies, and merely given a Korean dress.

CHAPTER 7

CONSERVATIVE ASIAN THEOLOGIES AFTER WORLD WAR TWO

ASIA THEOLOGICAL ASSOCIATION AND THE EVANGELICAL RESPONSE
The Asia Theological Association (ATA) was formed out of the concern that evangelicals had neglected theological scholarship in the past and that the Asian church leadership was increasingly being influenced by western liberal theology. First constituted in 1968 at the Asia South-Pacific Congress of Evangelism in Singapore, its primary goal was to develop 'evangelical scholars, thinkers and teachers for the leadership of the Church in Asia'. Theologically it represents main-stream evangelicalism.

With respect to the first criterion for a mission-based theology, that of relevance to socio-political concerns, ATA has moved from the traditional conservative position. Its 'Statement of Faith' speaks of 'the *total* mission of the church to the *whole man in society in the contemporary context*' (my italics). This emphasis on holistic mission is further elaborated in the 'Hong Kong Declaration', which states:

> We are burdened with... Asia's need, a need with physical, social and political aspects as well as spiritual. We see ourselves as responsible for proclaiming the gospel in all its breath as well as its depth. We confess our past failures to identify with Asian man in his personal and social suffering.[19]

Moreover, personal conversion is not the end of the Christian life. Christian transformation has to be brought into the socio-cultural sphere.

Writers within ATA have begun to wrestle with some of these issues, but having affirmed the importance of Christian social responsibility, the 'Hong Kong Declaration' nevertheless goes on to emphasise the primacy of evangelism:

> Until men are brought to put their trust in Jesus Christ as Lord and Savior, God's good news has not come home to them in any biblical and meaningful sense. We must bring men under the challenge of the gospel so that their lives may be transformed by the power of God and they may be built up in

the fellowship of God's church. In giving priority to evangelism we emphasise the transcendence of God.[20]

With respect to the third criterion of inculturation, there are both strengths and weaknesses in the ATA. It has made serious efforts to relate the gospel to the different Asian religions and cultures and this is clearly seen in the consultations organised on defining theology within the different Asian contexts, the question of Christianity and ancestral practices in Asia, and the doctrine of God in the midst of Asian religious plurality.

However, little has been done to go beyond the efforts of the Chinese theologians of the 1920s. Few examples can be found wherein the relation between the gospel of Christ on the one hand, and Chinese culture, philosophies and religions on the other, are explored seriously in the manner of the early Christian apologists, to show that Christ is relevant to the deepest longings of the Chinese heart.

On the negative side, it has to be noted that the thought of many Asian evangelicals still betray the captivity of their worldviews to the Enlightenment rationalism and western dualism. This can be seen in ATA's continuing prioritising of evangelism over socio-political transformation despite its formal commitment to holistic mission in its 'Statement of Faith'.

Although some within the ATA take Hiebert's 'excluded middle' and power encounters seriously, many Asian evangelicals have been just as rationalistic as their more liberal counterparts. In the extreme cases (although not ATA itself), Christ's power to heal has been denied in the name of dispensational theologies which speak of the cessation of the gifts of the Holy Spirit today. Fortunately, this resistance to the ministries of healing and exorcism is now fast breaking down, in part due to the Pentecostal-charismatic challenge.

A third example is found in ATA's formulation of the nature of the Bible, which speaks of it as 'infallible, and inerrant'. This shows that its understanding of biblical authority and inspiration is not really different from that of much of western evangelicalism, which centres on the concept of 'inerrancy'. It appears that a much sounder contextual approach is to root the authority of scripture in God who can be trusted to speak truthfully about himself, and in Christ who bears truthful witness to his Father, and whose revelation comes with its own self-authentication. This shifts the emphasis from one centred on *conceptual analysis* to one centred on our *relationship* with and our *experience* of God. This, incidentally, is the same way in which Calvin defended the authority of the Bible when he affirmed that 'Scriptures must be confirmed by the witness of the Spirit'. Asian evangelicals, despite the problems they have with Koyama's theology, can learn from him when he affirms that 'the finality of Christ' cannot be proven by mere rationalistic objective methods. We 'see' when we are given 'extraordinary' sight.

We come finally to the fourth criterion, that of faithfulness to the Christian tradition. ATA represents a basically orthodox Christian position. At the same time, there is a recognition within the leadership of the need to develop a much more contextual theology. For example, it has been said that the ancient Christian creeds were not 'designed for the challenges that confront the church in Asia today'. Hence, there is the need to develop an 'Asian confession of faith' which is both living and seeks to relate the biblical historical faith to today's life and challenges. While genuine beginnings have been made in this direction, generally speaking, the ATA and related writers have remained largely within the western evangelical mould in their theological formulations.

To sum up, ATA theology is strong on evangelism and pastoral concern. Theologically, it is basically orthodox and its efforts in inculturation should be rated as fair, but because its theology is still largely held captive to western categories it is still fairly weak in its socio-political thought.

VINAY SAMUEL (1939-) AND HOLISTIC MISSION

Vinay Samuel was trained in India and undertook graduate studies at Cambridge. He is a presbyter of the Church of South India, and from 1982-85 he was also the Vice-President of the Karnataka Central Diocese of the church. He has worked in various forms of evangelistic, parish, social outreach and theological training ministries in India. Further, he is closely associated with the Theological Commission of the World Evangelical Fellowship (WEF) and the Lausanne Movement and has been the Executive Secretary of the International Fellowship of Evangelical Mission Theologians (INFEMIT).

Samuel's ideas have often been worked out together with others, and many of his papers are co-authored with the British scholar Christopher Sugden. Samuel's theology is first and foremost an evangelical reflection on mission among the poor in the Indian context. However, unlike some others, his convictions emerged out of personal involvement at the grassroots level of day-to-day ministry to the poor in India. As part of this process, for some years he moved his family out of a middle-class environment to live in Lingarajapuram, one of the slums of Bangalore.

Out of this background, Samuel came to the perception that the meaning of the good news in the Bible for the poor defines the meaning of the good news for all. He writes:

> *The focus of the poor demonstrates the nature of the reality of the gospel which is meant for all … In the New Testament, the poor … (is) the focus of the gospel. As the poor are called; as the multitude rejoice and experience the gospel, the real nature of the gospel becomes evident to others. This in no way means that the gospel is not for other groups. It does mean that it has to be mediated through what it means to the poor. Its fulness could only be appreciated when its nature was revealed through this marginalised group.*[21]

In other words, for Samuel, 'The agenda for the middle-class church must be the agenda of the poor'.

This leads to the second distinctive in Samuel's theology. Sugden calls him the 'Theologian of Dignity.' In India, there exists an integral relationship between the social structure, caste system and Hindu religion. The resulting poverty robs the poor of dignity and a proper sense of identity. Thus, for Samuel, the concept of dignity is the key category, 'for interpreting the gospel among poor people, integrating his theological thought in the Indian context, giving an analytical perspective on Indian society, undergirding and directing his mission strategy and entering into dialogue with other religions.'[22]

Such a restoration of dignity, which frees from all dehumanising tendencies in the context of India, can only come through the gospel of grace. The gospel offers men and women an identity and dignity which is independent of their role, status and work. It comes from a new set of values which is rooted in our creation in the image of God as God's children. Thus, 'the search for an authentic Asian Christian identity is the crucial issue for mission in Asia today'.[23]

This leads to the third distinctive aspect of his thinking: the emphasis on holistic mission or 'integral evangelism'. For him, the relation between evangelism and social responsibility is not a matter of either/or, but one of inseparability. The prioritisation of humanity's vertical relationship over the horizontal presupposes 'a dualistic understanding of existence'. It assumes that humans live in two separate realms, an inner and an outer realm, with the former centred on our relationship with God and experienced individually, and the latter on the physical and social realm. However, this cannot be justified on either biblical or philosophical grounds. Therefore, conceptually we cannot separate personal and social change. The love of God and the love of the neighbour are inseparable.

It should further be noted that, for Samuel, holistic mission goes beyond holding evangelism and social action together. It also involves taking Hiebert's 'excluded middle' seriously. Since oppression has both human and demonic roots, it therefore requires a response which draws on every level of the biblical material. Thus, mission necessarily includes the work of the Holy Spirit in healing and exorcism ministries. By holding these different dimensions together as being integral to holistic mission, Samuel has gone a long way towards overcoming the dualism and rationalism that have plagued western theology for so long, and pointed the way forward to a genuinely contextual Asian theology.

As part of his overall concern for holistic mission, Samuel seeks to develop a coherent theory of social change from an evangelical perspective. For Samuel and Sugden, 'the church is central in any program of Christian social change'. Rejecting both the concepts of the 'open church' and the 'invisible church', they opt for an understanding of 'the membership and the mission of the church in terms of the Kingdom of God'. The church consists of those who are members of the kingdom who give their allegiance to the King and whose lives are ordered by the values of the kingdom. This approach sees God's kingdom active both in the church and the world.

Further, Samuel and Sugden reject a purely 'creation-based theology' of social change which fails to take the implications of Christ's redemption into consideration. Among other problems, this leads us back into a dualism wherein redemption deals with the spiritual and supposedly takes precedence over creation which deals with the merely physical. This is precisely what was rejected in the emphasis on holism already noted. Instead, they argue for a theology of social change which brings together the creation perspective with God's work of 'eschatological salvation which is present now'. This enables all efforts for justice and social change to be taken into account.

Samuel and Sugden warn us against tying our faith to any one particular mode of analysis or ideology. The Christian's task is not to avoid human ideologies and movements, but to present the gospel as the means whereby these can be redeemed from their most terrible perversion so that they do not betray but realise their true human ends.

How does Samuel's theology measure up by the four criteria for a mission-based theology? On the first criterion of socio-political responsibility, he cannot be faulted. His life, ministry and writings breathe with a concern for the poor. Moreover, in his writings he has consistently sought to advance the level of evangelical social thought.

On the second criterion of evangelistic and pastoral concerns, he can hardly be faulted either. Samuel's commitment to evangelism is transparent in his writings, and unlike ecumenical writers like Thomas, Koyama and Song, he unhesitatingly affirms the importance of personal conversion and allegiance to Christ.

The third criterion of inculturation is also taken seriously by Samuel. First, by affirming the importance of dialogue, he demonstrates that he takes the multi-religious context of India seriously, and refuses to allow his theology to be domesticated by the dualism and negative aspects of the Enlightenment paradigm which have plagued much of western Christianity. Further, he attributes the lack of holism to 'the process of demythologisation' (presumably advocated by liberal Christianity) and 'the spiritualisation of history' (presumably practiced by many evangelicals). These 'demonstrate the effects of the Enlightenment on Christian mission worldwide'. In fact, Samuel is one of the earliest to draw attention to the debilitating influence of the Enlightenment on thinking about mission.

Nevertheless, it has to be noted that despite his acceptance of the importance of the healing and deliverance ministries, there is little detail discussion of these in his writings. This suggests that he may not have sufficiently integrated the concerns of Hiebert's 'excluded middle' into his theology.

A third indication of his commitment to inculturation is his concern to balance the individual against the community. Unlike western approaches which tend towards individualism, Samuel consistently refuses to deal with the individual apart from the community. The person is first and foremost humanity-in-community. This is not only very Asian culturally, but soundly biblical as well.

Perhaps the most significant way in which he takes inculturation seriously is the manner by which he relates the salvation history of the Bible to that of the histories and cultural identities of all nations. When the Gentiles were invited into the community of God's people, they were invited despite their particular histories which they did not lose by becoming Christians. Rather,

> they were incorporated into the people of God and took the history of Israel and their Messiah as theirs also, not as replacement for but as an addition to their own national history. So the history of Israel was the history of God's promise to all the nations, and the promise to Abraham was likewise a promise for blessing to all peoples. Now in Christ all nations must relate their own histories to Israel's history and must incorporate themselves into it.[24]

Two conclusions flow from this. First, if the Gentiles do not lose their own national histories in becoming Christians, then their histories and cultural identities are important and crucial to the affirmation and recovery of their own Christian identities.

Second, if the Jews may not monopolise biblical salvation history, how much more should western Christianity not be allowed to do so! However, with their long Christian heritage, western churches have tended to see non-western churches as mere extensions of themselves. However, what unites non-western to western churches should not be the former's wholesale acceptance of western forms of Christianity. Rather, it ought to be 'their acceptance along with the churches of the West of the entire stream of Judeo-Christian history – even as they retain their own cultural history. This process is crucial for the discovery of African, Asian, or Latin American Christian identity'.[25]

Samuel asserts that the histories and cultures of the nations can only be affirmed when we insist both that salvation history is unique, and at the same time that it cannot be monopolised by Israel. Gentiles who enter the community of God's people have incorporated themselves into that history. In so doing, they will come to recognise that their own national histories find in God's biblical promises their final fulfilment. Samuel does not find it necessary to jettison a foundational theme, which lies at the heart of classical Christianity, as a precondition for non-western churches to discover their own identities in Christ.

This bring us finally to the fourth criterion, that of faithfulness to the Christian tradition. Samuel has consistently identified himself with the evangelical tradition which has always taken the question of theological orthodoxy seriously. Samuel does not hesitate to criticise traditional western evangelical theology, when that is called for, such as its dualistic prioritisation of evangelism over social concern. This is also true in regards to inter-religious dialogue. He believes that evangelicals are too hesitant here because of their fear of syncretism, being misunderstood, and the decline of evangelism. Further, he also chides evangelicalism, as represented in sections of the 'Lausanne Covenant', for showing little or no inclination to ask the question whether God is at work in other faiths. Instead, he urges that both for the sake of the social transformation (which in a religiously plural context cannot occur 'without a religious reality that promotes that change'), and for the effectiveness of our evangelistic approaches, serious dialogue is unavoidable.

At the same time, he is careful to guard against being sucked into the pluralist agenda. In a subsequent paper, Samuel lays down some clear parameters for an evangelical approach to dialogue and for relating to peoples of other faiths with integrity. These include a clear affirmation of the uniqueness of Christ in Christian revelation, the need to distinguish between Christ's own exclusive claims from those made by the institutional church, the willingness to discern the presence of God in others' religious experiences, the recognition of the sinful and demonic in religions, and to work wherever possible for the redemption of all creation. This approach clearly avoids two opposite dangers: that of extreme conservatism on the one hand which sees nothing good and redeemable in non-Christian religions, and that of present-day religious pluralism on the other which recognises no essential differences between the Christian and non-Christian faiths.

So what are we to make of the doubts raised about his orthodoxy? Samuel is committed to the evangelical tradition, but where it has fallen into cultural captivity, he wants to recall it to its primary commitment to the Bible and its missiological responsibility to proclaim its message within its context. Therefore, where necessary, he is prepared to challenge traditional western evangelical formulations and to move beyond them.

Thus, on the one hand, he firmly asserts 'the authority and objectivity of God's Word'. However, on the other, he warns us against trying to draw from scripture a set of timeless, universal truths. Rather, we are 'to seek by word and deed to embody in our context the words and work of Jesus'. Indeed, 'if we seek to proclaim one set of timeless truths in the Scripture in the same way to all men', we prevent people from understanding the gospcl.

Few would disagree with Samuel that the presentation of the gospel requires that it be contextually clothed, but whilst denying the possibility of 'timeless, universal truths', he affirms unambiguously that there are biblical themes which are transcultural. In that case, is he not trying to have his contextual theology cake and eat it at the same time? For if these themes are transcultural, then are they not in some sense 'timeless, universal truths' as well?

Beyond this, it is probably difficult to fault Samuel with respect to the fourth criterion for a missiological theology. Where he has gone beyond traditional evangelical theology, as represented by main-stream ATA thinking and others, he has done so in a direction which he and others believe is more faithful to the gospel of Christ. The particular strength of his position is that he has affirmed all these within the context of a hermeneutical approach which takes seriously cultural anthropology, sociology and the philosophy of language on the one hand, and the authority and objectivity of God's revelation in scriptures on the other. The former and the latter are often the respective weaknesses of evangelical and ecumenical theologies today.

To sum up, given some areas of weaknesses with respect to the third and fourth criterion, overall Samuel's theology is missiologically strong.

CHO YONG-GI AND THE PENTECOSTAL CHALLENGE

The last writer we will look at is Paul Cho Yong-Gi (1936-) from South Korea. Cho grew up first against the background of the Japanese occupation, and then the turbulent years of the Korean War. At 18, in the midst of an illness, he was converted. Soon after, again in the midst of illness, he had a vision of Christ and received his calling to preach the gospel. He trained at the Assemblies of God Bible College in Seoul and, except for a brief stint in the army in 1961, has been ministering since 1958.

Today he pastors the largest church in the world, the Yoido Full Gospel Church in Seoul, which by 1994 had a membership of some 700,000 members. He also spends about half his time ministering internationally. He may well be the best known Pentecostal minister in the world today.

Although not a theologian, the very fact that his is the largest church in the world does require us to give him a hearing. More importantly, one of the basic premises of this study is that theology must be pastoral and mission-based. With numerous books in print, and many of them translated into multiple languages, Cho is probably more widely read than any of the other theologians studied in this book. Cho is as influential in the Asian church as any of the academic theologians studied here, and his work poses fundamental challenges to the more academic theologies that we have been looking at.

Theologically, Cho stands in the evangelical tradition. To this he adds the Pentecostal characteristics, the most notable of which is the emphasis on the Holy Spirit's power to do 'signs and wonders'. For him, 'without signs and wonders, the church cannot grow'. He writes, 'I just read the Word of God diligently and apply the principles contained therein to my own ministry... I have seen souls saved, broken hearts healed, physical diseases touched by the power of the Holy Spirit.'

But beyond this Cho has some distinctive ideas of his own. First, the Christian message is one of 'hope', which he defines in terms of 3 John 2, 'I wish above all things that thou mayest prosper and be in health, even as thy soul prospereth'. For him, this refers respectively to the three aspects of a person: the spirit (the part wherein God is present), the physical body, and the soul (the human personality). Salvation is holistic: it includes the salvation of the soul, the healing of the body and material blessings from God – a 'triple salvation'.

For Cho, it is the fourth dimension of the spiritual realm which controls the third dimension, the physical. All humans have both the third and fourth dimensions in their hearts. Satan also has access into the fourth dimension. This explains why non-Christians, magicians and Satan can effect miracles in the physical realm. The Christian can also access this realm in order to change circumstances in the physical world. This can be done through 'faith incubation' and prayer.

What is 'faith incubation'? Like a baby who needs to be incubated in the mother's womb for a period of time before it is born, prayer goals need to undergo the same process. The four basic steps of this incubation process are 'envisioning a clear-cut objective', 'having a burning desire', 'praying for assurance', and 'speaking the word' to show evidence of faith. Through 'faith incubation' in prayer, we will then be able to see God acting miraculously in healing, material provisions, and so forth.

How does Cho's theology measure up missiologically on the basis of the four criteria we are using? First, with respect to the first, Cho is not known for his advocacy of active socio-political action. During the difficult years of military dictatorship in the 1960s through to the early '80s in South Korea, he kept away from the anti-government protests. Success, after all, whether spiritual or material, comes through prayer and not public dissent. On the other hand, there is a strong social concern in his ministry, including caring for the elderly, vocational training for underprivileged, and financing hundreds of open-heart surgeries for children. And since 1987 the leadership of Cho's church has begun to pay increasing attention to socio-political needs and challenges in Korea.

On the second criterion of evangelism and pastoral concerns, Cho is clearly very strong. 'Winning souls' is the highest priority in his work. Church growth is fundamental to his concept of mission. For this purpose he set up Church Growth International in 1976 to promote methods learned at Yoido Church world-wide. At least one observer has noted that despite his denial in his book, *More than Numbers*, numbers do mean a great deal to him.

There are probably four key elements in his church-building method. The first is prayer, as exemplified by the regular and extended prayer sessions at Yoido Church and especially, at the 'Prayer Mountain'. The second is his emphasis on the power of Holy Spirit in working 'sign and wonders', which shows that he clearly takes Hiebert's 'excluded middle' seriously. The third is the extensive use of home cell groups for evangelism and pastoral nurture. The Yoido Church is divided into more than 60,000 cell groups meeting regularly each week. The fourth is his development program for lay-leadership. By giving serious attention to this, he shows the seriousness with which he takes the New Testament understanding of 'body life' in the church, and develops it into an effective program of pastoral oversight.

Coming to the third criterion of inculturation, it is clear that in some ways Cho is still very much captive to a western dualism. This is seen, for example, in the priority of evangelism over everything else. Yet in other ways he has been accused of over-accommodating Korean culture.

First, some western observers have remarked that Cho's leadership is very authoritarian, paternalistic, and centred too much around one person. In response, it ought to be said that this observation applies to many other Korean church leaders. This in fact is an expression of the leadership patterns that is found in Confucian cultures in general. However, the question that needs to be asked here is whether behind this criticism lies the hidden assumption that only a western democratic pattern is 'right'? Further, given the cultural patterns of Korean society, would an imposed western leadership style work? Clearly the answer to both is 'No'.

Perhaps the more appropriate question to ask would be whether Cho has in anyway challenged Korean cultural patterns of leadership by the New Testament doctrine of the 'priesthood of all believers'. In at least one place, he has clearly done so. Within the strongly male-dominated Korean society, he has allowed women into important leadership roles in his church. Here then is a clear example that he is not selling out to Korean culture. That being the case, would it not be better for us to leave it to Cho and the Korean church leadership at large to sort out for themselves how best to maintain a proper and creative tension between biblical principles and their own cultural patterns in such matters?

A more troubling accusation is that Cho has allowed Christianity to be 'shamanised'. This accusation focuses especially on his healing and exorcism ministries, and the promise of earthly blessings. With respect to the former, I believe the criticism is misplaced. Rather, Cho's work in this area is an excellent example of how the gospel must be appropriately contextualised to address the felt needs of a people. In his own words, he is consciously seeking 'to show the miraculous power of God *to those who still believed in shamanism'* (my italics). The very admission by one of his critics that, 'The only difference is that a shaman performs his wonders in the name of spirits while Rev Cho exorcises evil spirits and heals in the name of Jesus' would seem sufficient to clear him on this point.

However, what about earthly blessings? Writing about both Cho and others, Son Bong-Ho explains that, 'The main temptation is to emphasise the promise of earthly blessings in order to attract the shamanistically attuned Korean populace'. Two comments appear necessary in response. First, Cho initially formulated his ideas at the beginning of his ministry among a mostly poor and uneducated populace, emerging out of the deprivations of the Japanese occupation and the horrors of the Korean War. Against this background, the question must be asked as to what sort of God is the Christian faith proclaiming if he cannot be called upon to provide 'our daily bread'? As we have earlier noted, for Cho salvation is not merely a spiritual matter.

Second, Cho has attempted to clarify his own position in response to the charge that he is preaching an American 'prosperity gospel', which is very similar to shamanism at this point. According to him, prosperity does not merely mean money. Rather, the oriental understanding is different. 'Prosperity is successfully fulfilling the goal God has set for us.' Financial gain or loss is not the most important, so long as God's goal is achieved. Nevertheless, it is doubtful that Cho has adequately shown that his 'oriental' understanding of prosperity is really different from that of the American version. Myung argues that his theology is weak on sanctification, and that it must include a much stronger emphasis on sacrifice and self-denial if it is to avoid ending up as 'another typical health and wealth gospel contributing to self-centred dreams'. Or, to put it in another way, Cho has yet to convince his critics that his grasp of the theology of the cross is firm enough to free him from the temptation to shamanise the gospel, in relation to material blessings, to attract greater numbers.

This leads us to the fourth criterion, that of faithfulness to the Christian tradition. Again, a number of questions have been raised against Cho. First, Cho has been accused of teaching that, 'it is God's will for the sick to be healed and that healing will come if one prays with faith'. To be fair to Cho, this is not exactly where he stands. He himself has also had to struggle with unanswered prayers for healing. His solution is that we should only ask after having waited on God and received a *rhema*, a specific Word from God, concerning his will about the matter under consideration. If it is not his will then we cannot force God's hand simply by asking. This is clearly orthodox, but what is not clear is whether he is coherent and Christian on some related points.

It is difficult to avoid the conclusion that there is an element of incoherence running through different parts of his theology. Thus he argues that we should not be too concerned about numbers, yet numbers are everywhere in his writings. 'Prosperity' is not just about financial success, but financial success does feature very strongly in his teaching and is drawing lots of people. One cannot force God's hand in healing, yet if God does not heal it is probably that the supplicant has not prayed enough, or repented enough, or lacks the necessary faith. Despite the talk about holiness, there seems little emphasis on personal sin and repentance.

It appears that at the root of the problem with Cho's theology here is a strong experience-centeredness, reinforced by cultural influences (both Korean and American) on the understanding of success and prosperity. This has led further to a tendency to oversimplify his theology. The combined effect of these is to prevent Cho from allowing his theology to be more fully moulded by Christian truths, especially the cross.

How missiological is Cho's theology? He is clearly very strong with respect to evangelism and the pastoral building-up of the church. In his thought and work, elements of inculturation are clearly present, as evidenced by the Pentecostal emphasis on 'signs and wonders' which takes Hiebert's 'excluded middle' seriously. However, in prioritising evangelism over everything else, he reveals his captivity to western dualistic thinking, and there remain questions whether he is over-accommodating Korean culture at some points. With respect to his theological beliefs, they are generally orthodox, but they appear to need more careful and reflective interaction with biblical truths to prevent his Christianity from degenerating into an experience-centred and self-centred religion.

However, what of the relevance of Cho's theology to the question of empowerment for socio-political change? It is clear from our analysis that Cho is reasonably strong on social concerns which seek to alleviate human suffering at the micro-level. What is also clear is that, unlike the *minjung* theologians, he shows little interest in active advocacy for socio-political change at the macro-level. Cho's theology clearly needs a deeper grasp of the socio-political implications of the gospel of Christ. Thus missiologically, on this it can at best be rated fair.

However, at this point we need to raise an important question. The above analysis of Cho appears to confirm the common perception of Pentecostalism as 'the haven of the masses', offering an escapist religion against a background of socio-political oppression. However, some recent studies have indicated that such a characterisation of Pentecostalism is too simplistic and in need of revision.

While Cho needs to have a deeper grasp of the socio-political implications of the gospel, and his weakness reflects his captivity to dualistic thinking, yet there remains the possibility that his Pentecostalism may have at least as strong an impact on socio-political transformation in Korea as *minjung* theology has, if not more! For, apart from the evidences adduced from studies on Pentecostalism above, there are other evidences and arguments which clearly show that evangelism and pastoral nurture of

Christian converts into strong counter-cultural communities are not disparate, but complementary, to more pro-active approaches to the process of social change.

CONCLUDING REMARKS ON SOME TRENDS
OBSERVED IN PROTESTANT ASIAN THEOLOGIES

We are now in position to sum up the overall trends in Asian theological writings that have emerged from our study. To begin with, except for Niles, ecumenical writers generally take the socio-political dimension very seriously in their theological endeavours. Conversely, conservative writers are traditionally much weaker here. However, evangelicals have increasingly come to take this dimension much more seriously. This is particularly true of Samuel, but also of some others. In general, it would be fair to say that ecumenicals are generally much better represented in areas involving advocacy for social reform and political activism. On the other hand, it is almost certain that evangelicals are at least as well represented as ecumenicals, if not more so, in the grass-root ministries of social concern for alleviating suffering.

With respect to evangelism and pastoral ministry, we see the reverse trend. Again with the exception of Niles, the ecumenical writers are weak, and the conservatives strong. The same trend is seen in their ecclesiology. Whereas Thomas, Koyama, Song and *minjung* theologians are vague about the faith-commitment boundaries of the church, conservatives would insist in general that there must always be a conscious owning of Christ as Saviour and Lord.

In relation to the concept of the Holy Spirit's power in the life and ministry of the church, while evangelicals do affirm it unhesitatingly, it is the Pentecostal Cho who, more than anyone else studied here, has thrown down the gauntlet to the Asian church to fully appropriate the biblical teachings on the power of the Holy Spirit in the work of evangelism, healing, exorcism and pastoral care. The ecumenical writers, Thomas, Koyama and Song also speak of the power of the resurrection in their theologies, but invariably this tends to be interpreted socio-politically, especially in terms of the redemptive power of God as revealed in 'the powerlessness of the cross'. Although there is an important truth here, which should also serve as a corrective to the Pentecostal-charismatic approach to power to prevent it from becoming triumphalistic, in itself it is nonetheless a very limiting approach to the understanding of God's power in the world. After all, to take one example, Luther's concept of the *theologia crucis*, which Koyama is so rightly fond of, also contains a very strong emphasis on *Christus Victor*, a feature which is not at all prominent in Koyama's theology.

On inculturation, almost all those studied here will claim that they are taking it seriously, in their respective ways. For example, the ecumenical writers, Thomas, Koyama, Song, and to a lesser extent, Niles, have sought to enter into an in-depth dialogue with Asian religions. Conservatives may disagree with their approaches and results, but, with the exception of Samuel, their hesitation to wrestle with the deeply perplexing questions of God's activity outside the Judeo-Christian tradition will hinder them, not only from taking non-Christians with seriousness and integrity, but also from fully incarnating the biblical faith in the Asian soil. On the other hand, some of the efforts made by the ATA, like seeking the best ways to express our understanding of God in the midst of Asian religions, have within them the beginnings of a more fruitful Christian apologetic and a more contextualised theology in Asia.

Nevertheless, as we have noted, in different ways the various theologies continue to reveal their captivity to the presuppositions of western dualism and the Enlightenment. With the exception of Samuel, each writer or group tends to split evangelism and social transformation, reflecting their dualistic presuppositions. With the exception of Cho, Samuel, and some within the ATA, they fail to take Hiebert's 'excluded middle' zone seriously, thus betraying their secularised Enlightenment worldviews. The same is true at the theological level. Apart from Niles, the ecumenical writers tend towards a liberal non-dogmatic Christianity. On the conservatives' side, the preoccupation with, for example, 'inerrancy' shows their domestication by Enlightenment rationalism, as if the problem of spiritual and theological authority can be solved by human reason alone.

Finally, with respect to faithfulness to the Christian tradition, we noted that conservative theologies are generally orthodox, but are still very much entrapped in the cultural and philosophical categories of the west. On the other hand, ecumenical theologians have been rather ambivalent about the question of faithfulness to the apostolic tradition. Except for Niles, there is an explicit dislike for dogma, and there is almost total ambiguity about the content of the 'irreducible core' of the gospel. This leads to further denials of crucial elements in the Christian tradition.

Going from Niles, to Thomas, Koyama, and then to Song and the *minjung* theologians, one sees an increasingly liberal trend. Whereas Niles, Thomas and Koyama affirm the uniqueness or finality of Christ in some way or other, Song can only speak of Christ's 'decisiveness', but even then reduces the meaning further by speaking of it in terms of 'degrees of truth'. Niles and others affirm the unique nature of Israel's salvation history and challenge the historical understanding of the Hindu-Buddhist worldview with it. In contrast, Song reduces biblical salvation history to the same level as all other histories which he deems to be equally salvific, apparently by interpreting it according to the Chinese understanding of history. Finally, Niles asserts a 'weak' salvation universalism but with clear boundaries for the church and affirmation of the importance of evangelism. With Thomas and Koyama, evangelism is secondary, explicit confession of the name of Christ is not particularly relevant to salvation, and the preference is for an 'open church' with blurred faith commitment boundaries at best. Further, in the case of Koyama, there is almost certainly an implicit pluralism. By the time we come to Song, we find an explicit salvation universalism and a clearly implicit pluralism. And as for *minjung* theology, there are genuine questions as to whether it takes seriously the crucial elements of the New Testament faith.

With the one possible exception of Samuel's, underneath the Asian 'clothes' and 'colours' that have been given to these theologies, we have found layers and layers of Enlightenment and dualistic thought. It appears that mature examples of a truly contextual Asian theology have yet to fully emerge.

CHAPTER 8

TOWARD AN ASIAN CHRISTIAN THEOLOGY

In this concluding chapter I would like to tentatively sketch out the 'contours' of a truly contextual Asian Christian theology.

Recent discussions on hermeneutics and contextual theology often revolve around text and context, action and reflection. The text is the Christian tradition based on canonical scripture and interpreted in light of the ecumenical creeds of the first millennium. The context consists of the socio-political setting, the evangelistic and pastoral ministries of the church, and the cultural-religious milieu. Action concerns the mission of the church, in evangelism and church-building, healing and exorcism ministry, and socio-political action, all of which should properly be interpreted in light of the Kingdom of God theme, but action also leads to theological reflection, and a purely speculative and theoretical approach to theology is rejected for a number of good reasons. It is untrue to the way theology has emerged in the Bible, and in most periods of church history, and in much of the two thirds world today. Splitting theory from practice is neither Christian nor Asian and academic approaches which fail to be rooted in pastoral and missiological practice distort theological analysis and reflection.

LITERARY GENRES REQUIRED IN ASIAN THEOLOGY

Theology comes to us in different kinds of literary forms. We see this in the variety of literature found in the Bible itself: the biographical and historical (historical books and gospels), the hymnic (psalms), the didactic (prophetic books and epistles). In church history, theology has been done through art, music and song, letter, biblical exegesis, biblical exposition and sermon, apologetics, systematic theology, and so forth. All these require reflection in a true Asian theology.

Biblical Exegesis

Furthermore, if the Bible has such a central place in in Christian reflection, the Asian church must take its interpretation seriously. Presently in Asia, there is a problem here. On the one hand, there have been a number of outstanding evangelistic and pastoral figures whose writings are widely read by the church. These include Sundar

Singh of India, and Watchman Nee and John Sung of China in an earlier generation, and Cho Yong-Gi of Korea today. However, generally speaking, their approach to the biblical exegesis tends to be rather simplistic, literalistic, and sometimes even allegorical. On the other hand, we also have a lot of commentaries and expository writings imported from the west, with all the associated presuppositions that we have already noted. Neither approach is the most desirable. The former is helpful to Christians in dealing with the daily problems of the Christian life, but fail to help them come to a deeper grasp of the message of the Bible in its totality. The latter may be academically and even theologically profound, although that is not always the case, but does little to help Asian Christians relate the gospel to real life because of their alien backgrounds.

One observer has drawn attention to the need for the development of a proper Asian Christian hermeneutic which would incorporate some of the wealth of textual studies in Asian cultures over the past two and half millennia. This is no doubt a very needful process, especially when it comes to in-depth interactions with Asian cultural and religious thought. For the moment I would simply draw attention to something more basic. Asian Christians must begin to learn to read and understand the Bible from within their own contexts, shorn of dualistic and Enlightenment presuppositions.

To begin with, we must strive for a more holistic (in contrast to dualistic) reading of the Bible. Asian cultural dimensions can also help provide insights into the message of the Bible. For example, western readings of the Bible often emphasise guilt, rather than shame. This is important in understanding truths like justification. However, what about the Parable of the Prodigal Son (Luke 15:11-32)? To read it from the perspective of sin and guilt draws attention to the twin themes of repentance and forgiveness. Nevertheless, it misses something crucial. Only when we understand the *shame* that the son's act has engendered for the family in the setting of an Asian (or African) village, and the fact that the father has totally 'lost his face' in the eyes of the whole community, with nowhere to hide it, can we begin to grasp the costliness and the depth of the divine love in the heart of God.

Another example comes from the episode of Saul's visit to the witch of Endor (1 Sam 28:8-14). Because western Christianity generally fails to take Hiebert's 'excluded middle' seriously, commentators always seem to have problems with the key verse: 'When the woman saw Samuel, she cried out...' (v.12). The straightforward explanation would involve taking the whole spirit world seriously, and also recognising that the ban in the Bible against medium practices is based in part on the fact that this involves trafficking with demonic powers rather than genuine ancestral spirits. Thus, the witch of Endor was shocked when Samuel appeared because that was the last 'spirit' she expected to see. As it is, all sorts of exegetical gymnastics are employed, including revisions which grossly violate the integrity of the text, to try to explain away a passage that seems incomprehensible, and thus missing its real meaning altogether.

What the above examples demonstrate is that Asian Christianity can make serious contributions to the church's understanding of the message of the Bible. This is a challenge that the Asian Christians should take up more seriously.

Christian Apologetics

Apologetics in the history of Christian theology means the defence, by argument, of Christian belief against external criticism or against other worldviews. While there have been further developments in theology in general, there have been relatively little serious apologetics written in recent years. However, the Sri Lankan theologian, Lynn de Silva, has written a most interesting book, *The Problem of the Self in Buddhism and Christianity* (1979). Without going into detail here, he has accomplished not only an able exercise in dialogue, but also a brilliant Christian apologetic addressed to Theravada Buddhists despite his intentions, thus showing that his careful and sympathetic understanding of another religious tradition can open new doors for meaningful communication.

Systematic Theology

Another genre that needs to be developed is systematic theology. Due to what the term connotes, this may sound surprising, with some questioning that if linear logic is not the primary mode of thinking of many Asians, should theology then be 'systematic' in an Asian context. Yet the preference for linear or non-linear logic is never exclusive in any culture. Rather, it is a matter of relative emphasis. Furthermore, modern science and education are so based on linear logic that its importance will inevitably grow, even in cultures where the traditional preference has been for non-linear forms of logic.

Second, the term 'systematic theology' sometimes implies in the western theological tradition the idea of some principle or philosophical concept, but what is envisaged is a *systematic* reflection on the key themes of the Christian faith arising out of a interaction between text and context, informed by mission and pastoral concerns.

Asian Christians need a framework within which to think about God's revelation of himself and his activity in the world, in the context of their own cultures and the mission task they face. Unfortunately, there is not at present a single text in this field written from within Asia. Thus, almost every Asian seminary still uses systematic theology texts written in the west.

What would be a suitable approach for the development of such systematic theologies? One suggestion is to begin with the study of the development of the early Christian creeds, against historical and contextual backgrounds. These creeds, especially the Nicene and Apostles' Creeds, and the Chalcedonian formula, were the first 'systematic' formulations of the Christian faith which the early church was forced to undertake both to ward off heresy and to instruct its members. Such a study will enable us to see how the apostolic faith that was being handed down through the scriptures and traditions was contextually shaped in the process of its formulation by the early church. Having examined that in detail, we can then proceed to ask how the same process might be carried out afresh in the various Asian contexts today. This approach will ensure that the development of systematic theologies in the various Asian contexts will take both the text and the context seriously.

In the formulation of such theologies, the following goals must be borne in mind. First, like Calvin's *Institutes*, they should serve as catechisms for Christians and help them to better understand God's revelation of himself in the scriptures. Second, they should help Christians to think and reflect upon their faith in the context of Asian societies, with all their wealth of cultures and traditions, struggling to come to terms with modernity. Third, they should aim at nurturing Asian Christians in their spiritual growth and maturation process. Fourth, they should serve to inform and enhance the church's mission and pastoral practice.

For these goals to be attained, theological reflection must make a serious effort at relating the message of the Bible to the cultural context and the ministry of the church. I will illustrate this with examples.

Ancestral Practices

Earlier we noted that ATA held a seminar on this subject which affected many churches in Asia, including those in Confucian cultural realms. The importance of this matter for these churches is underscored by the historical fact of the rites controversy, which is still not satisfactorily resolved today. Chinese ancestral rites, for example, have both a religious and social significance. To participate in it in its original form does involve a religious act which, as it appears to me, would conflict with the demands of the gospel. However, to neglect it all together would rightly incur cultural condemnation of being disrespectful to parents.

For example, because of their beliefs Christians often feel that funerals should not merely be times of mourning, but also of rejoicing. However, often the lack of overt mourning within a culture that demands it, has led to comments actually overheard at a funeral such as, 'It is better to die as a dog than as a Christian.' A systematic theology within the Chinese context must deal not only with the question of how loyalty to God means non-participation in ancestral worship, but also of what functional substitutes need to be put in its place to demonstrate the Christian's commitment to a cultural value of highest importance within Chinese society.

When one thinks in terms of healing, exorcism and the miraculous, much has been said earlier to show the crucial importance of Hiebert's 'excluded middle' in the thinking of Asian peoples. This means that systematic theologies in Asia must ask and answer different questions from western ones. For example, western theology invariably asks the question: are miracles possible? This of course addresses the Enlightenment problem of a closed universe. In much of Asia that is a non-question because the miraculous is assumed and fairly regularly experienced. The question rather is: who or what lies behind a particular miracle? After all, healings and exorcisms occur regularly in temples, through the hands of mediums, shamans and others. Thus our theology must help the Christian to discern the true from the false, the actions of God from those of demonic powers, and genuine healings from those that lead the supposedly healed into deeper spiritual bondage.

In terms of church leadership patterns, often western denominational structures have been foisted onto Asian churches on the assumption that these are sacrosanct. This is particularly true when these involve sacerdotal or semi-sacerdotal views of ordination and leadership. The problems that result from this conflict of cultural assumptions are aggravated further when they are interpreted theologically. There is obviously a need to wrestle afresh with how Asian cultural patterns and Christian principles can be brought into a more creative tension with each other, so as to produce the desired kind of leaders for the Asian church.

Ethics

A further genre of literature that must be developed further is ethics, both personal and social. Christian personal ethics as taught in the Asian church are essentially the same as that developed in the west, and whether conservative or liberal, they are inadequate for the Asian church. For example, western Christianity presupposes that decision-making centres around the individual, hence principles take precedence over relationships in moral decisions. Yet group solidarity and relationships are crucial in Asian cultures. Thus, as we noted earlier, what may be considered nepotism elsewhere may appear morally justifiable, or even required, in a relation-centred ethic, where family ties are so close.

Another illustration of this tension is found in Walter Trobisch's exposition in the African context on the importance of 'leaving' before 'cleaving' in marriage. He rightly emphasises that theologically and emotionally, 'Only the one who has 'left' regardless of the consequences, and only those who 'cleave' exclusively to each other, can become 'one flesh'.' However, what he appears to have neglected is the need to remind married couples that due attention must also be given to the larger web of in-law relationships in cultures where group solidarity is fundamental. Thus, it is perfectly satisfactory for a newly married western couple to move into their own home – indeed it may even be culturally required – but in many Asian situations it may not be culturally acceptable and is often not financially viable. What shape then must 'leaving' take in such situations? It is questions of this sort that are in need of serious attention.

However, we need to go beyond personal ethics into a correct theology of social ethics and social engagement. Earlier the contributions of MM Thomas and Vinay Samuel have been outlined, and whatever their strengths and weaknesses, at least they have made determined pioneering efforts in this direction. What may be hoped for is that out of these will emerge a coherent theology of social change that will holistically integrate the spiritual, personal, and physical dimensions of human existence.

Such a theology would, like Thomas, take seriously Christian programs of socio-political action, the relation between human ideologies and the gospel, and co-operation with those who are not Christians. It would also, like Cho Yong-Gi, take seriously acts of mercy which alleviated day-to-day human suffering. It would further, like Samuel, strongly emphasise evangelism within the context of holistic mission. It will also go one step beyond and ask what the implications of the defeat of the 'principalities and powers' have for social change, and what is the place of prayer. Such an ethic should aim at helping the church understand the intrinsic relationship between the theology of the Kingdom of God and our responsibilities for the world. It would go a long way to move Asian Christianity out of its tendency towards self-preoccupation with the spiritual realm and into active social engagement as a fundamental Christian duty.

The need for this in Asia is clear. A Christianity that is based on social withdrawal can only open itself to the charge of irrelevance, as for example in China in the 1920s. Unfortunately, in many quarters both in and outside the church, this perception persists – although this picture may be changing, in part due to factors outside the church's control. To take just one example, Christians in certain Asian countries live under dominant Islamic control. With the growing Muslim pressures for religious territoriality and the extension of the *Shar'iah* (Islamic law) over everyone in such states, non-Muslims find themselves increasingly reduced to second-class citizens, marginalised socio-economically, and left with restricted religious freedom. It is in part against this background that Lamin

Sanneh has castigated western Christianity in its present interactions with Islam for losing sight of the gospel as public truth, which Islam would not do, and urged the need for its recovery. If we are concerned with freedom, dignity, human rights for all (whether Christians, Muslims, or those of other religions, east or west), the Christian cannot afford to withdraw from the 'public square'.

THEOLOGY FOR AND FROM THE GRASSROOTS

Finally, a serious effort must be made to bring theology down to the grassroots level of the church. One non-Christian academic, in private conversation, has observed that most of the Asian theologians today are writing for the academic world. A change of orientation is needed. This involves writing much of the material discussed above with the needs of the laity in mind.

However, more than that is required. Earlier we discussed the need for biblical exegesis to be done from an Asian perspective, although Bible commentaries are more likely to be read by the elite than the average Asian Christian. For the latter, there is a much greater need for more popular biblical expositions and sermon materials. Asian Christian leaders, both past and present, like Sadhu Sundar Singh, Watchman Nee, Cho Yong-Gi, have focused more on producing materials of this kind. However, the exegetical basis of much of these has often been found wanting. What is needed is much more of such materials dealing with pastoral issues, aimed at the instructing and edifying those at the grassroots, but built upon a sounder exegetical basis.

Furthermore, since Asian cultures do not function primarily with linear logic, literary genres that use other patterns of reasoning and knowing must be employed in making the gospel relevant to the local needs. This includes, for example, learning from Luther and Wesley the use of hymns for teaching sound theology – Niles' effort with the *EACC Hymnal* was a good beginning. Another example of such a concern is the effort being made in the church in China, with the assistance of Trinity Theological College, Singapore, to collect and publish indigenous Chinese hymns set to tunes using traditional musical instruments.

Another field of literature that can yield much fruit are biographies of great Asian saints of the last one-and-a-half centuries, like Pastor Hsi and John Sung of China, and Sundar Singh and Nehemiah Goreh of India. The biographies of these that are available at the moment are usually written from the western missionary's perspective, and addressed to a Western audience. No adequate biography of any of the above named persons, from the Asian church's perspective, exists at present. What is needed are more critical biographies written by those who fully understand and sympathise with the cultural backgrounds of these saints, which can convey to the Asian church today something of the struggles of such persons in their desire to live as God's people in their cultures and times. These will invariably help to give Asian Christians today a clearer sense of identity, so that they will not always be looking to the west (as many sadly continue to do) for models of theological endeavour and Christian leadership.

UNEARTHING HIDDEN PRESUPPOSITIONS
The arguments for authentic contextualisation in this book rest first and foremost on identifying the hidden presuppositions behind much of western theology which in turn have influenced almost all Asian theologies. The task of developing authentic Asian theologies in the future will need further explorations and refinements of the work already done at the level of western thought and theology.

There is much need for more in-depth work on Asian cultures and worldviews. This is particularly true with respect to the established literary cultures of Asia whose penetration by the gospel is still little more than skin deep. These include the Confucian cultures of Japan and China, the Hindu culture of India, and the Islamic societies. For example, in the case of China, the problem is simply but cogently put by Chan Wing-tsit: 'So long as Christianity fails to come in contact with Chinese intelligentsia, it will fail to reach the nerve centre of the Chinese people.'

It was to the credit of the early church that it came to terms with Hellenistic culture at a deep level. The contributions of Paul, Justin Martyr, Tertullian, Athanasius, Augustine and others were indispensable to this process. This is something that Asian Christianity has yet to come close to attaining. Much of this is due to the negative view that missionaries have taken towards indigenous cultures in the last 200 years. This trend is being reversed. One way to accelerate this is for the development of a new generation of scholars who are not only well trained in the Christian tradition, but also deeply versed in Asian cultures, philosophies and religions. The dearth of such personnel is illustrated by the example of the church in my own country, Malaysia. Christians today form some 8% of the population in a country which is about 60% Muslims, who are politically dominant. Yet after hundreds of years of existence in a country which has long been predominantly Islamic, the church has only begun to think of producing trained Islamicists within the last few years.

If we are to have an in-depth understanding of Asian traditions and culture, this will involve in-depth dialogue with Asian religions, because culture and religion in Asia are so deeply intertwined. Such dialogue is necessary for three reasons: the importance of treating others with integrity and respect, the effective communication of the gospel across religio-cultural barriers, and the need to cooperate with those of other faiths in social change for the common well-being of all.

The current problem with Christian attitudes to other religions is that most Christians have fallen into one of two extreme positions, neither of which comes to terms with the biblical witness. The first, more conservative position predisposes towards total exclusivism, wherein all without explicit faith in Christ in this life are deemed to be eternally condemned. This position fails to take seriously the biblical witness of those who are not in the main-stream of the Judeo-Christian tradition. This includes the status of Melchizedek (Gen 14:17-20; Ps 110:4; Heb 5-7) and the Magi (Matt 2:1-12), as well as the apostles' preaching on the subject, when in Acts 17:30, Paul speaks of the fact that 'God has overlooked the times of ignorance', clearly referring to the period before the gospel was preached in Athens. By and large, evangelical writings have failed to come to terms with these strands of biblical teaching. On the other extreme are the thoroughgoing inclusivists who affirm universal salvation, and the pluralists who accept all religions as equally valid ways to God. Enough has already been said to indicate why these positions are also inadequate.

Serious progress will be made in our attitudes towards other religions if two questions can be seriously addressed from the perspective of those who desire to be faithful to the apostolic faith.

First, how do we think about the salvation of those who do not have explicit faith in Christ? It appears that the overall thrust of the biblical witness points to somewhere between a totally exclusivist position and a thoroughgoing inclusive one. Second, how has God worked in the lives of those who are not Christians? If we take the position that God does not work in such lives, then we would appear to be denying what John (1:1ff) affirms through his *Logos* theology, or the doctrines of general revelation and providence, or the Wesleyan doctrine of prevenient grace. However, if we say that God works through the life, say of Gandhi, how do we discern where in his life God was, or was not, at work?

Conservatives in Asia have been slow to explore these questions, either because they start from an unbending exclusivist position, or because of fear of being labelled as unorthodox. In contrast, ecumenical writers have wrestled with these much more boldly, but their tendency to ignore the propositional dimension of the Christian faith has left them with no clear criteria by which to address these issues meaningfully. Real progress will happen when we transcend these limitations.

A fourth concern that must be taken into consideration are the insights of cultural anthropological studies. A number of important studies from different sectors of the church have emerged in recent years dealing with the relation between contextual theologies and cultures. These studies have consistently drawn attention to the need to 'listen' to cultures, and to pay attention to the relationship between cultural form and theological meaning. Yet hardly any Asian theological writings have seriously interacted with the questions raised in these studies, not least because there has not been sufficiently serious wrestling with methodological questions in the former. I believe careful attention to this area of studies will be necessary for further advances in our thinking on contextualisation. Let me give one illustration.

Earlier we noted, in our discussion of Vinay Samuel, that he and Chris Sugden echo the views of many in the field of contextual theology in affirming that there are 'no timeless truths'. I believe that this is correct in so far as we are thinking about the developed forms of theologies such as Aquinas' *Summa*, or Barth's *Church Dogmatics*. However, do we also mean by the phrase 'no timeless truths' that there are no truths that are understandable across cultures and time? If so, are we not thereby saying that no commonalities exist among humanity which stretch across cultures and time, and ultimately transcend them? If that is what we are affirming, will we not end up logically with a pure contextualism in which we can never be sure that the different contextual theologies share anything in common in our perceptions of God and his relation with us?

How are we to determine that which is timeless and transcultural in the midst of all that which is bound by culture and by time? I am not sure whether the present states of hermeneutical and cultural anthropological studies can provide a clear answer at this point, but it does appear that certain insights in cultural anthropology point in the direction of a solution.

The fact that Jesus died and came to life again in Jerusalem at a specific date some two thousand years ago is a historical symbol that is understandable across cultures and time. There are no cultures and there have never been a time wherein life and death are not understood. Other examples which have this quality appear to be relational in nature: 'God loves us', 'Christ died to reconcile us to God', and 'Christ defeated Satan at Calvary'.

The present suggestions are tentative and will need careful refinement and study by the Christian community. However, if we can narrow the core beliefs of the Christian faith down to a set of symbols wherein form and meaning are inseparable, and which also transcend culture and time, then we can have a means of establishing more clearly what is the 'irreducible core' of the Christian faith. After all, either 'Jesus is the same, yesterday, and today, and forever' (Heb 13:8), or he is not! I suspect that if the worldwide Christian community came to some agreement on such a set of beliefs after careful hermeneutical and cultural anthropological studies, it would probably look much like the sum of the key elements in the ecumenical creeds.

ADDRESSING THE CHALLENGE OF 'POWER ENCOUNTERS' IN ASIAN CHRISTIANITY

In various parts of this study, our attention has been drawn to the crucial importance of Hiebert's 'excluded middle' in Asian worldviews, and the necessity of 'power encounters' in the mission of the church. Throughout Asia, many of the liveliest churches, at least within Protestantism, exhibit to varying degrees 'charismatic forms' of Christianity. I use the phrase 'charismatic forms' of Christianity here to point out that these are not merely the products of the supposedly original charismatic movement from the west. It is true that the modern Pentecostal and charismatic revivals, which go back to the Holiness Movement and the Azusa Street Revival, have influenced Asian churches, but what is often forgotten is that many of the charismatic forms of Christianity in Asia have indigenous roots traceable to earlier Asian Christian leaders (people such as Sadhu Sundar Singh and John Sung), and also to the revival movements in different parts of Asia, which are at best loosely connected to the modern charismatic renewal from the west. However, what is rather distressing is that often the theological interpretations used by Asian Christians to understand the work of the Holy Spirit in their churches today have been borrowed almost wholesale from western Pentecostals and charismatics. This has led often to the importation of theologies which have little contextual appreciation of the Asian scene. Moreover, some of these theologies lack sound exegetical grounding in biblical revelation and proper historical theological perspectives, because they have emerged out of fundamentalist circles wherein careful scholarship is not always held at a premium. The resultant problems can be seen to some extent in Cho Yong-Gi's theology.

Many Asian Christians have been led by God to discover afresh the gifts of the Holy Spirit for themselves. They have learned to appropriate his power in addressing the vital issues of Hiebert's 'excluded middle', a realm which non-westerners often understand better than their western counterparts. This, together with other factors, has contributed to the vitality of much of Asian Christianity. Surely it is time for Asian Christians to dare to begin to formulate their own biblically informed understanding of the dynamics of the Holy Spirit's work!

That this is an important task was noted in our earlier discussion of Cho. He, among others, has challenge Asian Christianity to move boldly into the realm of 'signs and wonders'. However, to do so without getting lost in wild enthusiasm, exaggerated human claims, or even demonic deceptions, will require Asian Christians to do their own theological homework properly.

LEARNING FROM WESTERN CHRISTIANS

Finally, Asian Christianity must remember that much can still be learnt from our western counterpart. Despite the severe critique levelled here against the Enlightenment worldview and western dualism, and their insidious effects on Asian Christianity, I cannot share the views of those Christians who tend towards a distorted iconoclasm against everything western. Such a position is not only untrue historically to the contribution of western missions in the past, but it also involves a fundamental problem with respect to one's own Christian identity. It effectively says that as one who is a Christian as a result of the labours of those who, despite all their many weaknesses and failures, brought the gospel to Asia, I now assert that all that came together with that process and which made it possible in the first place is positively bad. The inner contradiction of such a position is plain.

Without going into details, it should be sufficient to note that the very fact that Asians approach truth more via relationship and experience, and westerners more via their rational faculties, is enough to demonstrate to us our need for each other to help us to come to a greater and more wholesome perception of the wonder and majesty of God. This and much more remind us that it is much more fruitful for east and west to learn from one another. How else can we experience the abundance and the wealth of the catholicity of the body of Christ? And how else can we finally bring into the 'Holy City' the fullness of 'the glory and honour of the nations' (Rev 21:26)?

Throughout Asia, there is a distinct awareness of a growing maturity springing up all over in the churches. Often the older sister churches of the west look with a sense of wonder at the vitality and growth of many of these, especially those in China, Indonesia, and South Korea. Increasingly, some churches like those in India and South Korea are sending out more missionaries than some of the traditional missionary-sending churches in the west. Clearly, the trends indicate that the Asian church will inevitably have an increasing role in Christianity worldwide in the twenty-first century.

Yet the fact remains that Asian Christianity does not have a very clear sense of its own self-identity. Moreover, as Koyama says, much of Asian Christianity is 'culturally deformed'. The overwhelming predominance of western culture in the modern world, and its consequent effect on the development of Christianity in the non-western world in the last 200 years, are generally accepted facts today. As a result non-western Christians in general, and Asian Christians in particular, have lost confidence in their own cultures and histories. Partly because of this, some Asian Christians have embraced Enlightenment categories which deny objective truth to religious beliefs. Consequently, as the pluralism debate and other trends indicate, they have lost confidence in the gospel of Christ as well.

Authentic contextualisation that takes seriously both Andrew Walls' 'pilgrim principle' and 'indigenising principle' demands a dual recovery of confidence, both in the gospel and in one's own culture and history. Without that, Christianity will never become fully incarnated in the Asian soil. When these are birthed by the grace of God, they will bring genuine blessings to the Asian church. They will give Asian Christianity a clearer sense of self-identity without which it can never fully mature and they will contribute to the healing of the divisions in Asian Christianity, much of which have been imposed from without. Finally, they will enable the churches in Asia to proclaim the gospel of the kingdom by word and deed with greater pastoral relevance and missiological fruitfulness.

ENDNOTES

[1] Ro, Bong Rin, and Eshenaur, Ruth, eds. *The Bible and Theology in Asian Contexts* (Taichung: ATA, 1984), 23.

[2] de Bary, Wm. Theodore, Wing-Tsit Chan & Burton Watson. *Sources of Chinese Tradition*, Vol.1 (New York: Columbia University Press, 1960), 115.

[3] LCWE. 'The Lausanne Covenant.' Statement of the International Congress on World Evangelization, Lausanne, 1974, reprinted in *New Directions in Mission and Evangelization, Vol.1, Basic Statements 1974-1991*, James A. Scherer and Stephen B. Bevans, eds. (Maryknoll, NY: Orbis Books, 1992): 253-259 (1974), Para.10.

[4] LCWE. 'The Willowbank Report.' Report on a Consultation on Gospel and Culture held at Willowbank, Somerset Bridge, Bermuda (6-13 January 1978), in *Down to Earth. Studies in Christianity and Culture. The Papers of the Lausanne Consultation on Gospel and Culture*, John R. W. Stott and Robert Coote, eds. (Grand Rapids, MI: Eerdmans, 1978): 308-339, Section 7d.

[5] Walls, Andrew F. 'The Gospel as the Prisoner and Liberator of Culture.' *Missionalia* 10:3 (1982): 93-105, 97f.

[6] Muggeridge, Malcolm. 'Living Through an Apocalypse.' *Christianity Today* (Aug 16, 1974):4-8, 5.

[7] Abraham, William J. *The Logic of Evangelism* (Grand Rapids, MI: Eerdmans, 1989), 95.

[8] Azevedo, Marcello de C. *Inculturation and the Challenge of Modernity* (Rome: Gregorian University, 1982), 11; cited in Arbuckle, Gerald A. 'Inculturation and Evangelisation: Realism or Romanticism.' In *Missionaries, Anthropologists, and Cultural Change,* Darrell Whiteman, Guest ed., Studies in Third World Societies. No. 25., Vinson H. Sutlive, et. al, eds. (Williamsburg, VA: College of William and Mary, 1984): 171-214, 193.

[9] Bosch, David J. *Transforming Mission. Paradigm Shifts in Theology of Missions* (Maryknoll, NY: Orbis Books, 1991), 454.

[10] Kaplan, Robert B. 'Cultural Thought Patterns in Intercultural Education.' *Language Learning* 16:1-2 (1970): 1-20, 15.

[11] Dye, T. Wayne. 'Towards a Cross-Cultural Definition of Sin.' *Missiology* 4:1 (1976):27-41, 36.

[12] Chao Tzu-chen, cited in Lam Lam, Wing-hung. *Chinese Theology in Construction* (Pasadena, CA: William Carey Library, 1983), 59.

[13] Lacy, Creighton. 'The Legacy of D. T. Niles.' *Internat. Bull. Miss. Research* 8 (October 1984): 174-178, 176.

[14] Elwood, Douglas J, ed. *What Asian Christians Are Thinking. A Theological*

Source Book (Quezon City: New Day Publishers, 1976), xxviii.

[15] Koyama, Kosuke. *Mount Fuji and Mount Sinai* (London: SCM, 1984), 259.

[16] Koyama, Kosuke. *Three Mile an Hour God* (London: SCM, 1979) 51-54.

[17] Song, Choan-Seng. *Third-Eye Theology. Theology in Formation in Asian Settings* (Maryknoll, NY: Orbis Books, 1979), 172.

[18] Song, Choan-Seng. *Christian Mission in Reconstruction – An Asian Attempt* (Madras: Christian Literature Society, 1975), 63.

[19] ATA. 'Hong Kong Declaration.' In *Voices of the Church in Asia. Report of Proceedings. ATA Consultation*, Hong Kong, Dec 27, 1973-Jan 4, 1974 (Singapore: ATA, 1975), 168.

[20] *Ibid.*, 167

[21] Samuel, Vinay, and Christopher Sugden. *The Gospel of Transformation*, unpublished mss., 30; cited in Sugden, Christopher. *A Critical and Comparative Study of the Practice and Theology of Christian Social Witness in Indonesia and India Between 1974 and 1983 with Special Reference to the Work of Wayan Mastra in the Protestant Church of Bali and Vinay Samuel in the Church of South India,* Ph.D. dissertation (U.K. Council for National Academic Awards, through Oxford: Westminster College, 1988), 232.

[22] Sugden, Christopher. *Ibid.*, 270.

[23] Samuel, Vinay. 'Mission in the Eighties. An Asian Perspective.' *Occasional Bull. Missionary Research* 4:2 (April 1980). 50-51, 50.

[24] 'God's Intention for the World.' In *The Church in Response to Human Need*, Vinay Samuel and Christopher Sugden, eds. (Grand Rapids, MI: Eerdmans, and Oxford: Regnum, 1987):128-160, 133.

[25] Samuel, Vinay, and Christopher Sugden. 'God's Intention for the World.' In *The Church in Response to Human Need*, Vinay Samuel and Christopher Sugden, eds. (Grand Rapids, MI: Eerdmans, and Oxford: Regnum, 1987): 128-160, 135.